The Sun Will Rise in the West

THE HOLY TRAIL

D0840538

The Sun Will Rise in the West

THE HOLY TRAIL

Es-Seyyid Es-Shaykh Taner Ansari Tarsusi er Rifai el Qadiri

Edited by Elizabeth Muzeyyen Brown

Ansari Publications
Napa, California

Editor: Elizabeth Muzeyyen Brown
Cover Design: Es-Seyyid Es-Shaykh Taner Ansari with Mushtaq Ali Shah and
    Elizabeth Muzeyyen Brown
Text Design: Shaykha Sheila Khadija Foraker with Elizabeth Muzeyyen Brown and
    Mushtaq Ali Shah

All quotes from the Quran and works by Abdul Qadir Geylani translated and interpreted by author.

This book does not imply any gender bias by the use of feminine or masculine terms, nouns and/or pronouns.

Library of Congress Card Number: 00-108558

ISBN: 0-9703185-0-2

Published by Ansari Publications
        PO Box 2511, Napa, California 94558, USA
        Fax: (707) 255-2587; Web page: www.qadiri-rifai.org; E-mail: qrt@qadiri-rifai.org

First printing, 2000
Printed in the United States of America
1 2 3 4 5 6 7 8 9 — 04 03 02 01 00

Bismillah er Rahman er Rahim
In the Name of God, the Most Merciful, the Most Compassionate

Preface

Bismillah er Rahman er Rahim

All praise is due to Allah, and may His peace and blessings be upon His Holy Prophet Muhammad and his family, and upon all of the prophets, messengers, our Pirs, our Shaykh, and all of the lovers of Allah who have helped smooth the way for those who follow. We wish to thank Allah for the opportunity to participate in the gratifying cause of sharing His light and love.

We begin this undertaking by glorifying the Exalted Owner of all Praise in the Islamic tradition, especially because this volume is based on spiritual inspiration. It is a brief synthesis of teachings on the Sufi path, culled from the vast repository of divine knowledge, and tenderly secured in the heart of Shaykh Taner Ansari. At the behest of his spiritual ancestors, Shaykh Taner's original intention in proffering this book was to introduce the basic philosophy and practices of Sufism to Americans. This objective came to include interested readers of any "Western" culture, or one in which the pervasive worldview is based on a tacit assumption of scientific and rational thought. It is particularly written for those unfamiliar with the principles of Sufism and/or Islam, although the subject matter indeed concerns those more fluent with such concepts and practices.

In Islam, women and men alike are enjoined to seek knowledge. In the Sufi view, a truly realized human being embraces "otherness" deeply; man becomes woman and woman becomes vii

man in the fruition of their common ground—humanness. In light of this, a stylistic feature in the writing which bears explanation is the consistent use of the masculine personal pronoun "he" throughout the text. We refer to Allah as "He," not because we conceive of God as a man, but for purposes of simplification. The Islamic word "Allah" connotes no gender. In Arabic, "*Hu*" is used when referring to Allah, and no equivalent exists in English. Sufis include all of reality within the concept of Allah, and therefore "He/She/It" would be more accurate, but clumsy when used repeatedly. Likewise, when referring to the human being, the masculine pronoun is used, rather than "he/she," "s/he," or some other configuration. Defaulting to the masculine usage for ease of reading is a matter of personal taste in style, and is certainly not derived from gender-bias.

As is customary in the study of Islamic spirituality, Arabic terminology is used throughout this text. This is done to optimize the conveyance of subtle shades of meaning in words which have no English equivalents. A "Glossary of Terms" is therefore available for quick reference. Also included is a list of "Suggested Reading and References" for further study on related topics of interest.

We suggest that the reader use this book as a springboard for meditative contemplation, the best of which, in the Sufi view, is done with an open heart. We invite you to partake of the content herein at a leisurely pace, as one would enjoy a bountiful feast. May this banquet of spiritual delicacies, served with affection from the heart of Shaykh Taner Ansari, delightfully nourish and bless yours.

—Elizabeth Muzeyyen Brown
Napa, California
May, 2000

"The Hour will not be established until the sun rises from the west, and when it rises (from the west) and the people see it, then all of them will believe (in Allah)."

—Holy Hadith of Prophet Muhammad

 This symbol is a calligraphic rendering in Arabic of "Peace and blessings of Allah be upon him," the traditional blessing on Prophet Muhammad, which Muslims utter after mentioning his name.

Introduction: The Message

Bismillah er Rahman er Rahim

This book is for the people of the West. One of the prophecies about Judgment Day is that before the end of the world, the sun will rise in the west. There is a twofold meaning in this. By "sun" we mean knowledge, the message of Allah. One interpretation of the prophecy is that Allah's knowledge will rise in the West before the end of human life on the Earth. The second interpretation of the prophecy is that the sun will literally rise in the west as a result of a major cosmic occurrence that throws the Earth out of its normal rotation, so that it will start spinning in the opposite direction. With this reversal will come the beginning of the end of the planet. However, Allah has assured us that He will not destroy any place or society until it gets His message and rejects it. He also promises that we will not be held accountable until the message comes to us.

Nearly all the prophets were born in the Middle East, because during those times it was the geographic and commercial center of the Earth's major civilizations. Because all major trade routes traversed this mercantile region, news was efficiently broadcast throughout the world when a message was sent there and then fanned out in all directions. The prophets were given the message in the language of the people who were the primary recipients, e.g., in Hebrew, Aramaic, or Arabic. From India to Europe, from

China to Africa, the roads converged in the Middle East, strangers commingled, goods and ideas were exchanged, and Allah's message was carried to distant lands.

We now live in an era of rapid global communication. The cultural crossroads has shifted to the West, where English is the dominant language. This book, an extension of the Quranic message which was originally sent in the Arabic language of an earlier era, is therefore written in modern English. Because of the massive migration to and colonization of the Americas in recent centuries, an enormous population in need of the message, and with the technology available to spread the message, awaits its arrival. Allah has thus chosen the West as the place to rise His "sun" anew. We are grateful that Allah has bestowed this favor upon us.

Allah created us with the ability to learn and to apply what we learn because he has chosen the human being to be His deputy. By implementing and applying the methods of science, we help to fulfill that duty. Through science, that is, by objective research, observation, and experimentation, we discover the truth about the nature of things. Science teaches us how we can adapt knowledge for our use, how we can avoid problems and improve our quality of life. It helps us classify things and understand systems and their interrelatedness. Open-mindedness is an indispensible trait for scientists in their quest for truth. When research is conducted with an open mind, we learn truths about our world. Moreover, Allah has always gathered spiritual leaders where science is most developed. This was the case in all of the great and influential empires of history, for example, in Byzantium, China, and India. As science and technology gain ground, so is the message from Allah more easily dispersed into the global community.

Allah sends information in terms that human beings understand. In times when the scientific grasp of things was not so sophisticated, Allah's message was conveyed in a conceptual framework which was familiar to the people of those eras. For example, the Arabs of Prophet Muhammad's (peace be upon him) time knew about animals—when they sleep, what they eat. They could therefore comprehend that the Prophet rode on a horse in his *miraj*, his famous spiritual Night Journey. People today have a better understanding than before of how our world works, how it is possible to fly in the air and run on water, because science has made sense of such things. Today, scientific concepts are widely understood, even commonplace. Our capacity to understand the message of Allah clearly and objectively has increased with the progress in science. That is why the sun is going to rise in the West.

We are all part of this rising sun. When we hear this message, if we make ourselves dip into and carry this knowledge, then we help to shine this light and are part of the sun that is rising in the West. The message is clear. It is the same one Allah has sent over and over since the creation of the human race. One, there is God, and God is powerful and superior to you. Two, there is you, and you are not god; you are under God's dominion and acting on earth in the name of God. Three, there is the rest of creation, the powers of God manifested in the universe. God has given us the key to be able to use these, to learn and know them. By doing this, we learn God Himself. That is why we are created: to know God, appreciate God, and find a means to love God.

The whole matter goes back to love. Allah wants to be loved. When we love someone, we love the eyes, the ears, the hair, the manners. Look at God—He has all of these stars. He very thoughtfully created you, and He wanted to show you the way, so He created the stars to guide you. He created rules and regulations, the laws of physics, chemistry, biology, all of this to show you what a great thinker He is, how much He is able to do. In return, He is expecting you to look, see, be amazed, and fall in love. That is the message.

You can be amazed by and fall in love with God if you turn your eyes away from yourself. This is why Allah created your eyes turning outward. Before some traitor invented the mirror, the message was clear: don't look at yourself, look at Me. It may take a long time to pry ourselves away from the mirror, because we have become so fond of looking at ourselves, but when we do, we realize why our eyes are naturally looking outward.

Everything in the universe is made in two ways: there are things within your control and things outside of your control. This is to prove that you are not in total control, that Allah's hand is over your hand. Wake up!

What must we do? We must praise Allah. Whether you see it or not, whether you believe it or not, everything in the universe is praising Allah. When you find the truth, you can see it. All things are praising Allah, by turning, by vibrating, by moving. So are you, all human beings, all of the animals, everybody. Your heart says *Al-lah, Al-lah, Al-lah*—this is how it beats.

Can you live without breathing? You cannot. Allah says in Quran-i-Kerim, "We put the summary of what you do around your neck." What do we have around our necks? There's a voicebox and an air passage. Each time we breath *hhhu, hhhu, hhhu*—this *hhhu* is the name of Allah, *Hu.* In Judaism it's *Ya Hu Wah,* in Islam, *Ya Hu.* You are saying His name whether you want to or not. This is the way your body makes *zikr*, the remembrance of Allah. Allah gave you the ability to control some things, and expects you to join the cosmos and use your body willingly, consciously, and knowingly by making *zikr*. Although you are already making *zikr* involuntarily, put your consciousness there now: *Hu, Hu, Hu*. Join in it and make it your own consciously. This is what Allah is expecting from you.

When you know the truth—that there is God and there is you—you have a responsibility to uphold the truth. Allah created the whole universe, including you, for a purpose. If you know your purpose, and act according to it, you will be in harmony with Allah's purpose and you will be happy. Happiness is centered in the heart. It is the heart taking control of the brain. If your heart is happy, everywhere else within you is happy. Allah says in the Holy Quran, "Hearts find peace only with the *zikr* of Allah." If you want peace in your heart, you have to make *zikr*. If you want peace in your brain, you have to surrender. Shut the mind up and surrender it to your heart.

The education of the brain, which is key, is the practice of inculcation. Keep saying that you are not god, there is some power over you, and things are going to happen the way He wants it to happen. It may be that it's also what you want, but it may be that it is not what you want. This is the Happening Chart: He wants and you want—it happens. He wants and you don't want—what He wants happens. You don't want and He doesn't want—it doesn't happen. If you surrender to Allah and look at things from His point of view, then you can understand Allah. You can join Him, and then things that you and Allah both want happen all the time. If that makes you happy, you'll be happy. But once you join Him, you may not really care what happens, because you see that what Allah wants happens anyway.

There is only one Life, and Life lives—that's His job. Life becomes a base for other attributes of Allah to manifest themselves. While living, Allah shows generosity, kindness, mercy, power, anger, patience, endurance, healing, whatever you can think of. Everything is based on Life, including love. Love is not in the dead, love is in the living. Life and love will not die. We are not here for the body. The body is just the means for us to experience Allah in the material world, where Allah can manifest His attributes in three dimensional forms, which become the solid proof of what we are thinking, what we want to do, or what we have done. With this proof we can be judged.

Allah is able to do all things. Carry this message, know Allah, adorn yourself with Allah's attributes, Allah's knowledge, and Allah's light. The biggest favor of Allah is to give His guidance, and He has given it to the West. Take advantage of it and hold on to it, so that you can take a path to Allah, straighten out your own life, straighten out your family life, straighten out your city life, straighten out your nation and all of humanity. If you want peace, love, blessings in your community, with no diseases and no fighting, you have to accept Allah's rights, which are the truth, as rights, His wrongs as wrongs, and apply them. When you apply them, you have the remedies for social, psychological, and physical illnesses.

Here is a picture of our present social situation:

In the San Francisco Bay Area, every sickness that you can imagine on earth exists. When the Indians were living in this place, they didn't have these sicknesses at all. We introduced them.

By handguns alone, fifty-two thousand people die each year in the United States. Kids are killing each other, not because they can get guns, but because they want to kill. If you take the guns away, they'll find something else to use.

Just in California, there are seventy thousand children born to unwed mothers each year. A city is added to California every year this way. Another prophecy about the time before the destruction of the world is that in the later times mothers and fathers will run away from their kids. They're running away now. So many children have only one parent; so many parents don't want to be responsible for their kids. Fathers often say, "I don't know, maybe this kid is from somebody else." Immediately they ask, "Are you sure it's mine?"

This is the picture we're living in. People kill each other for a pair of boots; you mean nothing to your friends but a dollar sign. Friendship can be profitable. Marketing tactics encourage you to use your friends right away, cash them in. Meanwhile, America represents itself to the masses by the likes of cartoon hero Bart Simpson and the monotonous violence of much of our popular music. This is our picture and it is the reason why we need knowledge, spiritual and scientific.

As so many civilizations before, we have reached a crucial point in our development, and how we act now will determine whether we take a quick path to destruction or manage to prolong our existence on earth. Knowledge is the truth. Truth prevails and falsehood vanishes. If you want permanence, you have to be after the truth. You can cheat yourself for a while, but in the end everything turns back to its origin. So, people of the West, take care of your sun, your light. The future of humanity depends on you. The longer you let this sun shine, the longer human civilization will survive. When the sun sets, it is the time for resurrection.

With heartfelt encouragement, we dedicate this book to you, the readers.

—Es-Seyyid Es-Shaykh Taner Ansari
Napa, California
May, 2000

The Sun Will Rise in the West

Contents

Preface vi
Introduction: The Message ix
1. The Concept of God 1
2. The True Human Being 9
3. The Word 21
4. Prophets and Messengers 31
5. Initiation into *Tariqa* 43
6. The Spiritual Administration 51
7. *Tasawwuf* 63
8. Fighting the Enemy Within 77
9. Surrender 91
10. Other Beings 103
Glossary of Terms 115
Suggested Reading and References 125
Acknowledgments 129
About the Author 133
About the Editor 133
Excerpts from *What About My Wood?* 134
Excerpts from *Between the Loved and the Beloved* 138

1. The Concept of God

Bismillah er Rahman er Rahim

Allah is the Light of the heavens and the earth. The analogy of His light is as a niche, and within it, a lamp. The lamp is enclosed in a glass. The glass is like a shining star, lit from a blessed tree, an olive neither of the East nor of the West, whose oil is almost luminous, though no fire touched it. Light upon light. Allah guides to His light whom He will. And Allah speaks to mankind in allegories, and Allah is Knower of all things. (24:35)*

The Sufi's goal in life is to achieve an intimate understanding of, and love for, God. As in any pursuit, he must have some idea of what he is looking for. The Sufi therefore asks, who or what is God?

The cornerstone of faith for all Muslims, including Sufis, is the statement "*La ilaha illa 'llah,*" that is, "There is no god but God." Muslims call God "Allah" because there is no gender implied in this Arabic appellation. Allah can have no gender because it would be a limiting factor, and Allah can have no limits. Muslims believe that God is omniscient, omnipotent, and is the uncaused Cause of all creation. Allah is without limit in every dimension, infinitely and eternally, the formless Creator of all forms. Allah is neither created nor can He be destroyed.

---

* This and all subsequent quotes from the Holy Quran are followed by numbers in parentheses, which refer to the chapter and verse of the citation. For example, (24:35) represents chapter 24, verse 35.

Modern physics gives clues as to the nature of this boundless Being. The one thing in the universe we know of that cannot be created or destroyed is energy. Energy can be understood as the capacity to do work, as the force which is behind all action, and as action itself. Energy is a kind of light/force, that which radiates and that which is radiated. It is both substance and movement.

For Sufis, because Allah is both uncreated and the Creator, Allah is the fundamental energy which has existed before all time. Furthermore, because Sufis believe that Allah is the Being who contains infinite knowledge and power to act in whatever way He wills, the Sufi concept of Allah includes His comprehensive consciousness. Simply put, Allah is the conscious energy of the universe, aware of and in command of all existence, unbounded by time or space.

Allah defines Himself in the Holy Quran as " … *the Light of the heavens and the earth*" (24:35). Just as we understand that light is energy, we conceive of Allah as energy. Allah as pure energy is formless, but contains the potential to create all forms. Allah's power is at once the energy used to create all forms, and the energy/substance of forms. We find the Sufi point of view supported by scientific research in the following statement: "'Light' creates our world of pattern and form. In agreement with many other scientists, we defined the domain for 'light' as the full range of the electromagnetic spectrum in modern physics theories. … Everything in the physical world represents various manifestations of light."[1]

For Sufis, Allah's inherent quality of awareness, His comprehensive and eternal consciousness, is another aspect of the "light" by which He describes Himself. From the perspective of the concept of Allah as the total and conscious energy of the universe, we can understand the declaration of faith "*La ilaha illa 'llah*" as a

---

[1] William C. Gough, "The Cellular Communication Process and Alternative Modes of Healing," p.8.

spiritual expression of scientific law. There can be no god but Allah, because the existence of any other power would limit God, Who is without any limit whatsoever.

With further investigation into the concept of Allah as energy, another notion emerges. If Allah is both the substance and the Creator of creation, there can be nothing else but Allah. There can be no place where Allah is not because that would imply that something outside of Allah, some other form of energy, exists. If another type of energy exists, it would limit Allah. Thus the Sufi understands his declaration of faith from the profounder perspective that nothing exists but Allah.

All creation consists of Allah's own substance. The basic matter of all things is contained within His singular reality. Sufis call this spiritual/material substance the Ninety-Nine Names or the Beautiful Names of Allah. These Names are Allah's diverse attributes, all of which comprise His entire Being. Allah's essence holds all of these qualities as potential energy. In the act of creation, His potential energy becomes kinetic.

Most of Allah's Names are found in the Holy Quran, interspersed in its many *suras*.[2] Sufis see them as Allah's way of describing Himself in the Quran, the Word of God revealed to Prophet Muhammad, *aleyhi salam*.[3] For Sufis, Allah's Names are the very stuff of creation, as well as the means by which Allah sustains it. The Beautiful Names, as compiled below, are understood by Sufis as a chart of universal elements which supersedes the periodic table of chemical elements devised by scientists.

---

[2] *Sura*: One of the one-hundred fourteen sections of the Holy Quran, sometimes translated as "chapter." Note: For ease of reading, most Arabic words used throughout this text wil be pluralized by using the suffix "s" rather than by using the more complicated, albeit proper, Arabic forms. Examples include *walis*, *qutbs*, etc.

[3] *Aleyhi salam*: Peace be upon him. It is traditional in Islam to send peace and blessings upon the prophets and archangels when their names are mentioned; abbreviated later in this text as *(a.s.)*.

The Beautiful Names of Allah

Allah's are the Most Beautiful Names. Invoke Him by them. And avoid the company of those who blaspheme His Names. They will soon be requited for what they do. (7:180)

Allah[4] — God
Ar-Rahman — the Most Merciful
Ar-Rahim — the Most Compassionate
Al-Malik — the Absolute Ruler
Al-Quddus — the Holy One
As-Salam — the Peace, Salvation
Al-Mu'min — the Believer
Al-Muhaymin — the Guardian
Al-Aziz — the Victorious
Al-Jabbar — the Compeller
Al-Mutakabbir — the Greatest
Al-Khaliq — the Creator
Al-Bari — the Shaper
Al-Musawwir — the Detailer
Al-Ghaffar — the Forgiving One
Al-Qahhar — the Destroyer
Al-Wahhab — the Giver, Bestower
Ar-Razzaq — the Provider
Al-Fattah — the Opener
Al-Alim — the Knower of All
Al-Qabid — the Constrictor
Al-Basit — the Reliever, Expander
Al-Khafid — the Abaser
Ar-Rafi — the Exalter
Al-Mu'izz — the Bestower of Honors
Al-Mudhill — the Humiliator

As-Sami — the Hearer
Al-Basir — the Seer
Al-Hakam — the Judge
Al-Adl — the Just One
Al-Latif — the Subtle One
Al-Khabir — the Aware
Al-Halim — the Soft One
Al-Azim — the Magnificent One
Al-Ghafur — the Forgiver and Hider of Faults
Ash-Shakur — the Thankful One
Al-Ali — the Highest
Al-Kabir — the Greatest
Al-Hafiz — the Preserver
Al-Muqit — the Watcher Over
Al-Hasib — the One Who Keeps Accounts and Measures of All Things
Al-Jalil — the Mighty
Al-Karim — the Generous
Ar-Raqib — the Vigilant
Al-Mujib — the Responder to Prayer
Al-Wasi — the All-Comprehending
Al-Hakim — the Wise
Al-Wadud — the Loving One
Al-Majid — the Majestic One
Al-Ba'ith — the Resurrector

---

[4] *Ismi Jalal* — Name of Might

Ash-Shahid — the Witness
Al-Haqq — the Truth
Al-Wakil — the Trustee
Al-Qawi — the Strong One
Al-Matin — the Enduring One
Al-Wali — the Protecting Friend
Al-Hamid — the Praised One
Al-Muhsi — the Appraiser
Al-Mubdi — the Originator
Al-Mu'id — the Restorer
Al-Muhyi — the Reviver
Al-Mumit — the Taker of Life
Al-Hayy — the Alive One
Al-Qayyum — the Eternal Caretaker
Al-Wajid — the One Who Forms
Al-Majid — the Glorious One
Al-Wahid — the One
Al-Ahad — the Unique
As-Samad — the Receiver of Requests
Al-Qadir — the All-Powerful
Al-Muqtadir — the Creator of All Power
Al-Muqaddim — the One Who Puts His Creatures Ahead
Al-Mu'akhkhir — the One Who Puts His Creatures Behind
Al-Awwal — the Before
Al-Akhir — the After

Az-Zahir — the Outer
Al-Batin — the Inner
Al-Waali — the Governor
Al-Muta'ali — the Supreme One
Al-Barr — the Doer of Good
At-Tawwab — the Accepter of Repentence
Al-Muntaqim — the Avenger
Al-Afu — the Forgiver
Ar-Ra'uf — the Clement
Malik al-Mulk — the Owner of All
Dhul-Jalali Wal-Ikram — the Lord of Majesty and Bounty
Al-Muqsit — the Equitable One
Al-Jami — the Gatherer
Al-Ghani — the Rich One
Al-Mughni — the Enricher
Al-Mani — the Preventer
Ad-Darr — the Creator of the Harmful
An-Nafi — the Creator of the Good
An-Nur — the Self-Emitting Light
Al-Hadi — the Guide
Al-Badi — the Originator
Al-Baqi — the One Who Remains
Al-Warith — the Inheritor of All
Ar-Rashid — the Capable of Right Judgment
As-Sabur — Patient One

Having briefly described the Sufi perspective on the nature of God, the next question naturally follows—why did Allah create the universe? We look again to Allah for the answer. In a holy tradition Allah told the Prophet Muhammad *(a.s.)*, "I was a secret treasure and I wished to be known, so I created creation." Allah fashioned the universe or universes from His pure light. His energy

THE MOST BEAUTIFUL NAMES
AND THEIR NUMEROLOGICAL EQUIVALENTS

existed in a formless state, and He willed the energy to take shape over time. In the act of creation Allah activated some of His inherent attributes, such as *Al-Khaliq*, *Al-Bari*, *Al-Musawwir*. Allah began the creation with one word, "Be." At that moment, the creation of the universe started.

The "Big Bang" theory of the origin of the universe corroborates the Sufi viewpoint. According to this theory, the universe came into being through a series of explosions. With each explosion a new chemical element was created. In Sufi terms, Allah's light thus began taking shape in material form, and the interaction of Allah's attributes produced variety and complexity. Waves, subatomic and atomic particles, molecules, cells, organisms, the development of all that exists began as energy and continues to exist as energy in various states of formation, from wave-particles to the human being. For the Sufi, the universe has long been understood as a many-layered totality, light wrapped in sheaths of increasingly more dense matter. Scientists now acknowledge the breakdown of the supposed barrier between light/energy and matter.[4] According to some, matter consists of "frozen light."

Allah's Names are manifest in various combinations at each point of creation. The formula Allah used for each thing determines its unique character. This uniqueness itself is an expression of Allah's name *Al-Ahad*, the Unique. Because Allah's intention was to be known, he created a being who could know Him intimately, as a living, conscious synthesis of His Beautiful Names. Allah designed only one creature to manifest all of His divine attributes. This fruit of the universe, the end-product of the creation of the worlds, is the human being.

---

[4] "Modern physics has already found that under the right circumstances in the quantum vacuum, light and matter can switch identities." Gough, "The Cellular Communication Process," p.8. For insight into recent scientific theories about the nature of light and matter, also see Gough and Shacklett, "Outer and Inner Light."

2. The True Human Being

Bismillah er Rahman er Rahim

All your creations and all your resurrections are to Allah as if it were a single self. For Allah is the Hearer, the Knower. (31:28)

Allah created the essence of human beings from His own essence. This is related to us in a *Qudsi-hadith*[1] in which Allah states, "I have created the soul of Muhammad from the light of my Countenance." Sufis understand Allah's Countenance to be His essence, from which He created the prototype human soul. Allah took light from His essence, and called this soul the *Nur-i-Muhammad*, or Light of Muhammad *(a.s.)*. "Muhammad" means "the praised one," so named because Allah was pleased with this original soul, which embraces all of His attributes. From this material Allah created the souls of all human beings. Therefore, the spiritual essence of human beings is from Allah, comprised of Allah's Beautiful Names.

Human beings were created to know and to manifest all of His attributes while living on this earth. He was created with the capacity to develop his humanness to an exceptional degree. Sufism is the method designed by Allah which enables one to become *insan-i-kamil*, a true human being who has realized intimacy with his Creator. When his spiritual potential has been

---

[1] *Qudsi-hadith*: Holy Tradition, i.e., a saying or action of Prophet Muhammad *(a.s.)* according to eyewitness accounts; also known simply as *hadith*.

achieved, a human being is fit to be Allah's representative, or viceroy.

Your Lord said to the angels: Behold! I am about to place a viceroy on earth ... and He taught Adam all the names.
(2:30, 31)

The human being has both an outer and an inner aspect. His inner self is an assemblage of four souls, the combination of which comprises the human spirit. These souls are energy-bodies, each of which originates in one of four spiritual worlds. Each soul has a specific location in the physical body. The finest, most rarefied soul, *ruhani ruh*, corresponds to the world of Allah's essence. This soul travels through three more worlds, taking on a covering from each of these worlds before it is complete. Each successive covering is made of denser material than the previous one. It is wrapped with the soul of the archangelic world, *sultani ruh*. Next it travels through the world of angels, visions, and dreams, and is wrapped again as the *seyrani ruh*. Then the soul travels to the body and is covered with the soul of life, *jismani ruh*. Each of the four souls of man maintains a relationship with the spiritual world from which it came.

The outer aspect of the human being is his physical body. The body is the final layer of wrapping, designed so that the human being can function in the material world. This body also comprises four separately classified entities: earth body, air body, fire body, and water body. Each of these bodies has unique properties, and combine as an aggregate in the human physical form. The *jismani ruh* is the soul which is connected to the physical body as a whole and gives it life. The human animal is a complex network of functions and systems, some of which are controllable, others not. For example, the blood circulates automatically throughout the body without conscious control, as the small intestine does its job of digesting food. On the other hand, healthy individuals can voluntarily move their limbs about, take a walk, or sing a song. Human beings normally have conscious contact with the *jismani ruh* and the *seyrani ruh*. One does not need spiritual guidance to see the body's energy at work, which is an activity of the *jismani ruh*, nor does one need spiritual guidance to have a psychic experience, which is an activity of the *seyrani ruh*. The consciousness of *insan-i-kamil*, however, is broader and deeper than normal. It is a fully ripened awareness of deep spiritual levels within the self, and a corresponding comprehension of multidimensional domains of universal reality.

Human beings have the unique capacity to make conscious contact with the spiritual worlds, and ultimately with the essence of Allah. *Insan-i-kamil* understands Allah, the universal reality, to a profound extent. By following the Sufi method he has developed mature consciousness of the reality of Allah. He understands that because Allah manifests Himself in everything that exists, even the deeply human way of knowing Allah's essence is really Allah knowing Himself in the human being.

The bridge between the outer and inner selves of the human being is the mind. The mind is like the command post of a ship, and is the seat of intelligent discrimination. It gathers data from within and without, then analyzes, judges, and makes decisions based on this data. Moral judgments can be based on external sources like the codified directives given to us by Allah through His messengers and scriptures, or may be arrived at inwardly, based on input received from the spiritual realms of the soul. Allah's name *Al-Adl*, The Just One, is manifest in the laws of scripture as well as in human consciousness.

Allah has fashioned the human being with the faculties of sense-perception so that we can experience His manifestation on various levels. To the outer man belong the five senses of sight, hearing, smell, taste, and touch. The inner man is also equipped with senses, or perception points, which act as receivers for information from the spiritual worlds. The ancient Jewish mystical system known as Kabbala classified these inner senses as the ten *sefiroth*. From one perspective, the *sefiroth* are understood as being attributes of God which He used in the creation process. Because God created man in His own image, Kabbalists were able to discern the places in the human body where the *sefiroth* can be found. Seen from this angle, the *sefiroth* are the inner senses of man, perception points which are both receivers of information and activators of God's powers.

> *But here are clear revelations in the hearts of those endowed*
> *with knowledge.* (29:49)

In Sufism, there are twelve or more perception points within the human being. The perception point which merits the most critical attention is the heart. Man's relationship to the highest world, the world of Allah's essence, is found deep within the heart. This secret place is where we meet with Allah face-to-face. It is where we come to know the unchanging reality, the Truth without form. This place is hidden behind layers of material, which pertain to both the spiritual and physical worlds. Sufis learn to unsheathe these layers one by one in the ancient process of purification called *tasawwuf,* known in the West today as Sufism.

The human being represents the full scale of universal reality, from the grossest physical substance to the highest spiritual mat-

SPIRITUAL PERCEPTION POINTS
AND CONNECTIONS*

1. The Crown
2. The Rational Mind *(aql)*
3. The Divine Soul *(sultani ruh)*
4. The Holy Spirit *(ruhani ruh)*
5. The Moving Soul *(seyrani ruh)*
6. The Corporeal Soul *(jismani ruh)*
7. The *Nafs*
8. Power *(Jalal)*
9. Mercy *(Jamal)*
10. Foundation
11. Steadfastness
12. Majesty
13. The Material World

*This chart is an augmented version
of the Kabbalistic system of *sefiroth.*

ter. Allah made the human being in this fashion so that he would
be a mirror of the universe, the microcosm which reflects the
macrocosm. A great Sufi saint, Mevlana Jalaluddin Rumi,
radiyallahu anh,[2] said, "If you want to know me, be me; if you
want to know love, be love." Firsthand knowledge of reality in
myriad dimensions is possible for the human being to achieve
because Allah designed him for that purpose. All of Allah's
Beautiful Names are contained within the human being. Free
will, the ability to make choices which can have wide ramifica-
tions for all of the earth's inhabitants, is the power that qualifies
the human being to be Allah's viceroy on earth.

Although humans contain Allah's qualities, human beings
are not Allah. Allah's reality is infinite, and all beings created by
Allah have limitations. Allah may expand a human being's capac-
ities to immense proportions, but Allah alone is the unlimited
Owner of all power, the one eternal reality.

Everything will perish except His Countenance. (28:88)

Because the human being was entrusted with more potential
than any other created being, one may wonder why human society is beset with so many problems, with social injustice, war,
poverty and the like. This complicated question must be
answered on many levels, not all of which are within the scope
of this study of Sufism. If we look more closely at the nature of
the human being, however, some answers may come forth.

Allah's quality of decision-making exists within the human
framework as the pivotal point in man's makeup. The ability to
discriminate, to make moral judgments and the like, implies that

---

[2] *Radiyallahu anh*: May Allah be pleased with him. In Islam, this is a traditional honorific phrase reserved for religious forebearers of very high spiritual rank; abbreviated later in this text as *(r.a.).*

Ascension depends on:

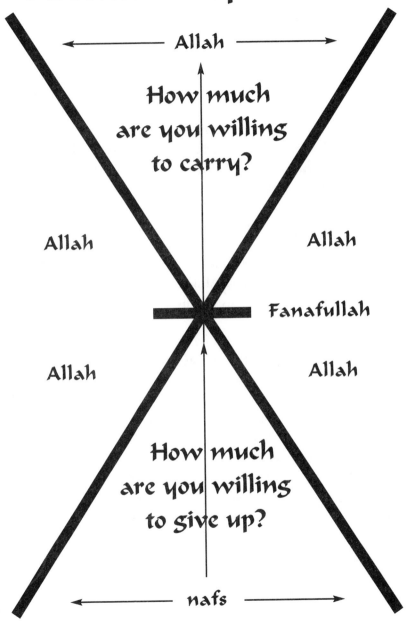

some actions are better than others. In all of His scriptures Allah confirms this, as for example in the Ten Commandments. If human beings were incapable of acting wrongly, their characteristic freedom of will would have no meaning. Allah endowed man with the ability to choose, then gave him guidelines to follow to enable him to make informed decisions.

In Allah's essence the contradistinction between good and evil does not exist because Allah is one reality. It is in the universal field of manifestation where duality appears, the place where Allah's names can be categorized as belonging either to the realm of His mercy, *Jamal*, or of His power, *Jalal*. Sufis conceive of the human being as a kind of trigger that activates Allah's mercy or His wrath. Good actions bring agreeable consequences, bad actions unpleasant ones. Although Allah exercises His justice, Sufis know that humans usually punish themselves, sometimes collectively.

The large apportionment of Allah's attributes given to the human being comes with commensurate responsibility. The actions of a single person can have far-reaching consequences, as, for example, in an executive decision to detonate a nuclear weapon. Everything that exists is essentially an energy-form, and the way in which this energy manifests affects all other energy-forms. Actions, thoughts, feelings, spoken words, all transmit vibrational patterns which produce reactions in the universe. Energy transmissions, as actions and thoughts of the human being, may be more consequential than he can fathom. They are not discrete or neutral. Rather, each thing in the universe receives the *Jalal* or *Jamal* consequences triggered by human behavior. Considering the relative mastery of the cosmic surroundings that humans enjoy, it is incumbent on them to act benignly and with good intentions.

*O you who believe! Be mindful of your duty to Allah, and seek the
ways of approach to Him, and strive in His cause in order that you
may succeed.* (5:35)

Prophet Muhammad *(a.s.)* said, "If you know your *nafs*, you
know Allah."[3] *Nafs* is an Arabic word which derives from the
word for "breath." Sufism simplifies the complex systems which
are involved in being human with the following formula:
Human Being = Allah + *Nafs*. Sufis understand the *nafs* to be the
material, ego-centered self. The *nafs* includes the body, with its
instincts and animal desires. All of the self-centered ambitions
which a person carries with him in life are considered part of
nafs. The sense of self as an individual apart from the whole is
nafs. *Nafs* can be seen as a negative entity which is an obstacle
between man and the oneness of Allah. This enemy does, however, have a positive function. Once we have learned to identify
the ways of *nafs* within ourselves, we have gained a perspective
from which to distinguish between selfish desires and the wishes of Allah. From this basis we may choose actions motivated by
the desire to please Allah.

A Sufi constantly strives to know whether his actions please
Allah or his *nafs*. In traditional Sufi terminology *nafs* is likened to
a donkey. The Sufi asks himself, "Am I riding the donkey, or is the
donkey riding me?" The method of Sufism is designed to help the
murid, a student of Sufism, identify his *nafs* so that he can con-
quer it. The point is for the *murid* to gain control over the *nafs*, so
that his actions and thoughts are Allah-based and not self-centered. When he succeeds, he achieves the optimum balance

---

[3] *Nafs:* This word, a singular form, has many shades of meaning. Whereas the
root of the word denotes breath, *nafs* is traditionally used by Sufis to describe
1. the whole man as an individual being; 2. man's ego, or self-centeredness; 3.
man's animal nature.

between his outer, material, self and his inner, spiritual, one. The Sufi's intention is to be in a continuous state of vigilance *vis-a-vis* his own *nafs*. In that way, he proves that he is choosing Allah and not himself. For example, *nafs* might incite him to cheat on an exam in school, but when he chooses not to cheat, he has shown that Allah's pleasure with his actions is more important to him than any temporary benefit derived from cheating. Having *nafs* is a natural and necessary part of the human condition; having one's *nafs* under control is the condition of the *insan-i-kamil*.

This material world is known as the world of proofs. In it, man has the opportunity to cultivate and demonstrate the strength of his determination to reach Allah's essence in this life. The intensity of the struggle with his *nafs'* desires is the standard Allah uses to judge man and reward his efforts with closeness to Him. The more choices made for Allah's sake, the closer man comes to knowing Allah. In exercising his free will in the right way, he learns to fulfill his destiny as a human being, to be a knower of Allah, His deputy, and, finally, His lover.

And those who strive to please Us, We surely guide them to our paths, for surely Allah is with those who do right. (29:69)

In the material world of proofs, Allah has made moral distinctions for human beings so that they can choose good and avoid evil. The wisdom on which good action is based is learned in three ways: by hearing of or reading about universal truths, by observing these truths in action in experience, and directly from Allah. It is Allah within that the Sufi strives to touch. Sufis wish to be with Allah in the same intimate way that lovers are united. All of creation serves Allah, willingly or unwillingly. Sufis wish to serve Allah willingly, knowingly, and lovingly. That is why Sufism is called the way of the heart, designed to bring the human being to his ultimate objective of loving intimacy with Allah.

We sent you not except as a mercy for all the worlds. (21:107)

When the heart is clean, the inner spiritual senses come alive to balance the outer senses. The mature Sufi's heart has become identified with Muhammad's *(a.s.)* heart, which is in constant rapport with the essence of Allah. It is aligned with Allah and the entire universe, and has, in a sense, become the universe. Through such a heart Allah sends His mercy to creation. The Sufi functions as a servant of Allah in this material world in an active way, through beneficial action, and in a passive way, as a conduit for Allah's mercy. In this way the Sufi is said to follow in the footsteps of Muhammad *(a.s.)*.

3. The Word

Bismillah er Rahman er Rahim

Say : Call upon Allah or call upon The Most Merciful, by whatever name you call (it is the same), for to Him belong the Most Beautiful Names. (17:110)

Allah defines Himself in the Holy Quran in terms of His attributes, the Most Beautiful Names. The Names are word-forms which encode their essential nature. The Names, and the word of Allah in general, act on a vibrational level in the arena of command, and on a symbolic level for instructional purposes. This two-fold function of the primordial word of Allah is, and has always been, played out in the creation and ongoing operation of the universe.

The Word as Command

For to anything, when We intend it, We only say the Word: Be! and it is. (16:40)

Allah started the creation with the word, *"Kun!"* which means "Be!" Words are one form of vibrating energy. From this initial commanding vibration commenced the secondary vibrations which interacted to produce the universe. From the perspective of

word-as-vibration, the whole universe can be seen as a book. It
is the book of creation, based on the word of Allah. The book of
creation is a universal system created within a framework of laws
and principles, both material and spiritual.

In the substance and process of creation one can see Allah's
essence as manifested in His Beautiful Names. For example,
Allah is *Al-Bari*, the Shaper, and *Al-Musawwir*, the Detailer.
Sufis perceive the universe as a matrix of energy-matter wrought
from Allah's attributes, issued forth from Allah's original command. The commanding power of the word is applied in the Sufi
method, in which the intrinsic power of Allah's Names is used to
promote spiritual advancement. It is a potent tool because the
key to this power lies in Allah's being, and is therefore used only
with His permission.

*Behold! When the angels said: O Maryam! Allah gives you glad tid-
ings of a Word from Him, whose name is the Messiah, Isa, son of
Maryam, honorable in the world and the Hereafter, and one of
those brought near to Allah.* (3:45)

An example of the commanding or creational power of the
word in human history is the person of Prophet Isa (Jesus) *(a.s.)*.
By Allah's command, the living being known as Jesus was created within the womb of his mother Maryam (Mary) *(r.a.)* without the biological intervention of a human father. Isa *(a.s.)* was
endowed with the ability to use the power of the word to bring
life to inanimate objects, to bring life back into people who had
died, and to heal infirmities. Such extraordinary deeds testify to
the tremendous capacity the word has to participate in ongoing
creative processes in our world.

Isa *(a.s.)*, along with other prophets and messengers, also applied the word in its instructional capacity, by communicating knowledge sent to mankind by Allah. These words are preserved in the holy books and scriptures.

The Word as Knowledge

And we have revealed the Scripture to you only that you should explain to them those things in which they differ, and that it should be a guide and a mercy for those who believe. (16:64)

Since Allah's whole purpose in creating the universe, or universes, was to be known, He chose to create a being who would embody His attributes of *Al-Khabir*, the Aware One, and *Al-Alim*, the Knower. He therefore created the human being with the curiosity and capability to understand the intricate workings of the realm of existence. In this way he could come to know and appreciate his Creator. In His mercy, Allah provided the means for humans to decipher the codes used in His creation. Language was developed, and words took on symbolic form as written figures. Words have been used as a means of communication between human beings and they have been used by Allah to transfer knowledge to us.

The human being was created with the great potential to understand Allah, bounded dually by the extent to which he chooses to seek this knowledge and by the Creator's liberality in its disclosure. Allah's attribute of *Al-Hadi*, the Guide, can be seen in the scriptures sent to mankind, in the prophets and messengers, and in messages received directly from Allah in the hearts of believers.

And it is not fitting for any mortal that Allah should speak to him, except by revelation or from behind a veil, or by sending a messenger to reveal what He will by His permission. For He is the Exalted, the Wise. (42:51)

The means used by Allah to transfer knowledge are threefold: *Ilm-al-Yaqin*, sure knowledge transmitted by verbal or written communication, *Ayn-al-Yaqin*, scientific or personal observation of sure knowledge, and *Haqq-al-Yaqin*, the revelation of sure knowledge by Allah directly to the believer's heart. *Ilm-al-Yaqin* is employed for the education of people especially when they do not have the advantage of a living messenger who can pass Allah's knowledge directly to them. It is general education for all people of all times. *Ilm-al-Yaqin* with *Ayn-al-Yaqin* are the means used by people living under the guidance of a prophet, by which Allah teaches them right conduct based on scripture and observed in the prophet's behavior. *Haqq-al-Yaqin*, in conjunction with *Ilm-al-Yaqin* and *Ayn-al-Yaqin*, is specific to Prophet Muhammad *(a.s.)*. Allah revealed truths directly to his heart, which were later confirmed by the archangel Jibril (Gabriel) *(a.s.)*. Muhammad's *(a.s.)* actions were based on this wisdom, which made him a living example for his people. These revelations were committed to writing for the education of anyone who seeks this knowledge.

The Books

It is He Who created the night and the day, and the sun and the moon: each (of the celestial bodies) floats in its orbit. (21:33)

Verbal communications from Allah which are committed to writing are known as holy books or scriptures and are an example of *Ilm-al-Yaqin*. The holy books mentioned by Allah in the Holy Quran are the Torah, the Psalms, the Gospel, and the Quran itself. Allah appointed messengers to receive and disseminate these scriptures, which demonstrate that He designed the universe and all of the beings within it according to a system of physical and spiritual laws. Directives for proper human behavior based on these laws are provided therein. For example, in the Ten Commandments Allah clearly delineates how He expects mankind to conduct themselves on the earth. He describes the type of behavior which is in healthy alignment with the human constitution and enjoins us to act within those parameters.

A scripture can thus be understood as an operational manual for human behavior, based on the universal schema of creation. When one behaves in compliance with the prescribed behavior, one's place in the universe is a harmonious part of the working whole. When one transgresses these laws, the consequences may not be favorable, to himself or to others. If a person should jump off a high cliff without a parachute, the chances are good that he will hurt himself badly, or even die. Painful repercussions may also be felt by his family, friends, and so on. We don't see his dying as a punishment, but rather as a consequence of reckless action with respect to the law of gravity. In spiritual as well as physical arenas, so-called "rewards" or "punishments" are actually the natural consequences of our actions. Because Allah is merciful and just, divinely sanctioned behavior turns out to be beneficial for us, as individuals and as a society. This is not to say that living on earth is all smooth and easy going, without hardships or obstacles for those who follow Allah's prescriptions. When a human being learns to see from Allah's perspective, what others may think of as negative or wrong, he may understand in a deeper way as being part of the larger order of things.

The Holy Quran

And this Quran is not such as could ever be produced by other than Allah; but it is a confirmation of (revelations) that went before it and a fuller explanation of the Book—therein is no doubt—from the Lord of the Worlds. (10:37)

The Holy Quran is the last scripture sent to mankind. It encompasses the earlier scriptures, acting as a kind of distillation of Allah's previously revealed precepts. The Quran operates on several levels, from injunctions regarding the most mundane of human daily experience to a portrayal of our cosmos, which has been confirmed in more recent times by scientific observation. There are moral mandates in the personal and social arenas, based on universal laws created by Allah, as well as teaching stories which refer to earlier civilizations, with lessons to be learned from their successes and failures. The Quran chronicles the entire history of mankind, from his creation to his demise on earth and his place in eternity.

And thus have We inspired in you (Muhammad) a Spirit, by Our command. You did not know (before) what the scripture was, nor what was faith. But We have made it a light whereby We guide of our servants whom We will. And surely you guide to a straight path. (42:52)

The single reason why The Quran is held to be the most important of revelations is the fact that it is the verbatim word of God. These words were revealed to Prophet Muhammad *(a.s.)* internally, by way of *Haqq-al-Yaqin*. The Quranic verses were shortly thereafter confirmed in the Arabic language to him by the archangel Jibril *(a.s.)* through *Ilm-al-Yaqin*, a process which was completed when Muhammad *(a.s.)*, who was not a literate man, delegated scribes to keep exact records. There have been no additions or deletions made to the Quranic text since it was originally revealed. An additional testament to its authenticity is the flawless lyrical and mathematical symmetry of its content. An uneducated person such as Muhammad *(a.s.)* could not have devised such an opus, which is considered the finest handiwork of Arabic poetic style, replete with intricate mathematical codes in the phrasing of its verses.

The teachings in the Quran embrace the spiritual and physical worlds and foster the realization that these are not separate domains. Rather, one learns that what we categorize as either the one or the other are really two sides of the same proverbial coin. Because Allah wished to manifest Himself, the material world was born, and what we call "spiritual" is simply a less solid form of the same energy which runs the cosmos. In Quran, the "inner" and "outer" aspects of reality meet. It is a complete manual of knowledge and behavior, an elucidation of good action based on correct intention.

Allah repeatedly and emphatically states in the Quran that the human being's time on earth is meant to be spent in acknowledgement of, and service to, his Creator. This is the demeanor of *insan-i-kamil*, what Allah intends him to be. Allah graciously fashioned man as a being who could know His infinite Being. The Creator asks in return only that man be grateful for this chance to partake of such bounty and that he act in a responsible manner concerning his allotment in life. Human beings are responsible for their actions because Allah has provided the knowledge on which to base them. The complex character of the human being reflects his embodiment of every one of Allah's beautiful attributes. Therefore man has the ability to wreak havoc and destruction on earth, as well as to promote a peaceful way of life. It is Allah's power of choice, free will, which man uses either to his advantage or disadvantage. The responsibilities which human beings shoulder are clearly laid out in the Quran. His first duty is to live a righteous life. Secondly, he must do his best to ensure his family's well-being. Thirdly, his actions should be beneficial to the community in which he lives, which extends in concentric circles through the world, encompassing the entire universe. It may be difficult to understand how a single individual's actions could have an effect on the entire universe. When we take into account the fact that energy is never lost in the cosmos, it is more easily comprehended. Using the observational method *Ayn-al-Yaqin*, we can perceive how this happens: a father shows cruelty to his son, his son in turn lashes out at those around him, and so on, creating a cycle of destructive behavior.

People who have attained a high degree of social leadership have a great obligation to act correctly, as their influence is felt more immediately and permanently on a larger scale. Humanity is even now suffering the consequences of some dictators' unjust wielding of power decades ago. Our society still has not recovered from the centuries-old legacy of the European-African slave trade. A human being is required to do his best to promote justice in the world. If he holds an influential social or political position, he must use that authority for the betterment of society. Those who are not in such position are obliged to use whatever power is at their disposal, be it their pen, their speech, or a sincere prayer. This injunction illustrates the importance of the proper wielding of the power of words, externally and internally.

And We reveal in the Quran that which is a healing and a mercy for believers. (17:82)

The beneficial effects of the Quran can be realized on the physical, moral, social, and spiritual planes, as the power of Allah's word operates on various levels which comprise man's inner and outer life. Deep spiritual insight which may result from a sincere reading of the Quran is an example of its efficacy regarding the inner man. It is said that there are as many as eleven levels of wisdom contained in the Quran. One learns to perceive these inner meanings as he progresses spiritually and taps into ever deeper areas of perception within his being. The apprehension of ever subtler dimensions of meaning within the Quran is an example of *Ilm-al Yaqin*, studying scripture, leading to the operation of *Haqq-al-Yaqin*, Allah's way of communicating knowledge directly to the believer's heart.

Reading the Quran has also been used to promote physical healing and demonstrates the profundity of knowledge inherent in this scripture. It is believed by healers who use the Quran as their medium that the vibrations produced while reciting certain passages procure the resultant curative effects. Numerological formulas inherent in the Quranic text are sometimes employed in the exacting procedures of spiritual healing. The physical impact of the commanding power of the word of Allah during the healing process exemplifies the conjunction of the inner and outer realms of existence in the human experience.

Outer and inner unity is consciously realized within the one whose knowledge, actions, and insight spring from the same unified source. The Sufi's aim is to internalize and externalize Allah's word in such a way as to "become the Quran." On this level, Allah's knowledge and commanding power, which are the two aspects of His word, have merged within the true human being. The model for the one thus fully realized is the Holy Prophet Muhammad *(a.s.)*.

4. Prophets and Messengers

Bismillah er Rahman er Rahim

Mankind was one community, and Allah sent Prophets as bearers of glad tidings and as warners, and revealed with them the scripture with the truth, to judge between people concerning that wherein they differed. (2:213)

Allah designated certain persons as His prophets, to be living repositories of direct knowledge from Him. As Allah's representatives on earth, the prophets (peace be upon them all) were obliged to consistently affirm the reality of the all-embracing dominion of Allah. They were sent as warners to people whose customs deviated from divinely prescribed behavior, in order to reinforce a sanctified relationship between God and mankind. The main vehicle for this sacred connection was the covenant, the ageless pact wherein human beings acknowledge the sovereignty of their Lord, who in turn reciprocates with His promise of divine guidance and protection. Allah established this spiritual contract in human society with Adam *(a.s.)*, whom He appointed as His first prophet. The divine covenant was subsequently renewed under the leadership of the prophets who succeeded Adam *(a.s.)* throughout the course of human spiritual development.

*Say (O Muslims): We believe in Allah and that which is revealed
to us and that which was revealed to Ibrahim, and Ismail, and
Ishaaq, and Yacub, and the tribes, and that which Musa and Isa
received, and that which the Prophets received from their Lord. We
make no distinction between any of them, and to Him we have
surrendered.* (2:136)

In the Islamic tradition, it is believed that there were one
hundred twenty-four thousand prophets sent by Allah to
mankind, although the deeds of many may not have been chron-
icled or may have been lost. Accounts of the teachings and
exploits of several prophets have been preserved in the holy
scriptures. Each of Allah's prophets were given a specific task,
with varying degrees of complexity and range. Some prophets
were given the role of warrior for establishing Allah's justice and
truth in a corrupt society. Others worked less visibly, as spiritual
protectors for their people through prayers grounded in their
intimate relationship with the Creator. Most of the prophets
were charged with duties limited to the particular society in
which they lived. However different the scope of each prophet's
task, whether they had two or two-hundred thousand followers,
believers are enjoined by Allah to acknowledge all of His representatives, to give them equal respect as bearers of His truth.

Common to all prophets was their role as conduit of divine
guidance and protection. Allah's light in the form of inner spiritual energy and outer wisdom was routed through them,
enabling the communities in which they lived to benefit spiritually and materially. The purpose of their lives, empassioned by
dedication to Allah's service, was essentially to be catalysts
through which the Creator fostered understanding of, and compliance with, the terms of the divine covenant.

Allah commissioned some of His divine emissaries to bring His message to the whole of humanity. Nuh (Noah), Ibrahim (Abraham), Musa (Moses), Isa (Jesus), and Muhammad (peace be upon them all), known as *Anbiya al Mursalin*, the Prophet-Messengers or Universal Prophets, were assigned the formidable task of transmitting divine knowledge deemed valid for all human beings of all societies. Allah commanded each of these prophets to reestablish and fortify the ancient covenant, based on the central proclamation that the one Supreme Being is omnipotent and is to be worshipped alone. The force of Allah's message sent through them was so powerful that it effected dramatic spiritual and social changes in their own communities and continued to expand throughout areas culturally, and often geographically, remote. The efforts of the Universal Prophets brought human civilization as a whole nearer to its full potential in spiritual relationship with the Creator.

The Universal Prophets each played a pivotal role in man's spiritual life on earth, and their descendants were often destined to be among the world's spiritual vanguard. Nuh *(a.s.)* was responsible for founding a new society based on the belief in one God after the great flood had obliterated the former civilization. Ibrahim *(a.s.)* was the instrument for the renewal of the divine covenant through his submission to the one God, foregoing the polytheistic errors which had crept into his ancestors' belief system. He became the progenitor of two major civilizations, Jewish and Arab, in which religious law was central to the societal structure. Musa *(a.s.)* was commissioned to unify and liberate the enslaved Israelites under the standard of religious law revealed to him by Allah. He was endowed with miraculous powers as an aid in his difficult undertaking.

The birth of Isa *(a.s.)* was a miracle in itself, as he was born of the virgin Maryam *(r.a.)* after Allah said the word and blew His spirit into her. His work was to reintroduce the essence of the true faith in one God, stressing the importance of love within his community grown rigid and corrupt under the influence of the Roman occupation of their land. Isa *(a.s.)* exemplified the union of the inner man with the outer, his ego having dissolved within the reality of Allah. A heretofore hidden path of oneness with Allah became manifest in society through him. He actualized the principles of *tasawwuf*[1] before the science of Sufism was formally revealed centuries later to Prophet Muhammad *(a.s.)*. Allah's mercy was manifested in his healing and creative powers. Through such apparent miracles, and because of the magnanimous nature of Allah which shone through him, this humble citizen without any political authority gained numerous followers among his fellow Jews. Although Prophet Isa's *(a.s.)* assignment lasted only three years, the message of the one God eventually spread with his teachings throughout the entire polytheistic, gentile Roman Empire and into Asia.

In the course of their work, some of the Universal Prophets delivered new mandates which augmented or otherwise modified the scope of the divine covenant in matters specific to particular situations. In some instances revised decrees regarding the outer aspects of worship were introduced, as, for example, in the formal structure of prayer or dietary discipline. The main task of those prophets who succeeded each of the Universal Prophets was to carry on his work by applying the updated law or lesson in their own communities. Aside from timely modifications of some of the terms of the covenant, the essential message remained constant as general counsel for all human beings:

---

[1] *Tasawwuf:* The system of spiritual cleansing known in the West as Sufism.

Believe in and worship the one God. Every prophet was charged with maintaining the believers' covenant of loyalty to Allah, with the promise to deliver His message and to help make the way for the next prophet's mission.[2]

Prophet Muhammad

Muhammad is not the father of any man among you, but he is the Messenger of Allah and the Seal of the Prophets; and Allah has knowledge of all things. (33:40)

The last prophet Allah sent to humankind was Muhammad of Arabia *(a.s.)*. He lived among a people taken to worshipping a variety of idol-deities, having fallen away from their original ancestors' faith in Allah. In his native Mecca, the Kaaba had been built centuries earlier by Ibrahim *(a.s.)* and his son, Prophet Ismail *(a.s.)*, as a sanctified destination for anyone who wished to venerate their Lord. By Muhammad's *(a.s.)* time, it was being used as a center for pagan worship and pilgrimage.[3] Social mores had likewise degenerated since Ismail's *(a.s.)* time. Reversion to polytheism had its counterpoint in the fragmentation of the tribal Arabian culture.

---

[2] *When Allah made (His) covenant with the Prophets, (He said): Behold that which I have given you of the Scripture and Knowledge. And afterword there will come to you a Messenger, confirming that which you already have. You shall believe in him and you shall help him. He said: Do you agree, and will you take up My burden (which I lay upon you) in this (matter)? They answered: We agree. He said: Then bear witness. I will be a witness with you. (3:81)*

And when We exacted a covenant from the Prophets, and from you (O Muhammad) and from Nuh and Ibrahim and Musa and Isa son of Maryam We took from them a solemn covenant; That He may ask the loyal of their loyalty ... (33:7, 8)

[3] Kaaba: Ibraham's *(a.s.)* House of God in Mecca has been the destination of Muslim pilgrims since the triumph of Islam in Mecca under Muhammad *(a.s.)*.

Interfamilial rivalry had become the norm, and loathsome practices such as female infanticide were common.

Muhammad *(a.s.)* never ascribed to the polytheistic beliefs of the majority of his people, and led a simple, meditative life. At the age of forty he received the call from Allah to be the last of His prophets on earth. For the first three years of his ministry he had a handful of followers, after which he received the command to spread Allah's light beyond his circle of family and friends. At the conclusion of his ministry the Kaaba had been restored to its original purpose, civil and moral standards based on Allah's prescriptions were in place, and the message he brought radiated throughout the Arabian Peninsula.

The spiritual energy housed in the person of Muhammad *(a.s.)* continues to abide in the world, more than a thousand years after he physically passed from this earth. At the beginning of the twenty-first century, Islam is the fastest growing religion in the United States and has more followers than any other single faith in the history of the human race.

Those who follow the Messenger-Prophet who can neither read nor write, whom they will find described in their Torah and their Gospel. He enjoins on them that which is right and forbids them that which is wrong. He makes lawful for them all good things and prohibits for them only the bad, and he relieves them of their burden and the yokes they wore. Then those who believe in him, honor him, help him, and follow the Light which is sent down with him: they are the successful. (7:157)

The first word Allah spoke to Muhammad *(a.s.)* was "Recite!" During a span of twenty three-years, the Quran was revealed to its living exponent, Muhammad *(a.s.)*, precisely so that man could learn in detail how to live righteously and in harmony within Allah's domain of creation. The first revelation to the Prophet *(a.s.)* indicates that Allah considers knowledge to be a priority for believers.[4] This fact is also borne out by several *Qudsi-hadiths*. The following are a sampling of the Prophet's *(a.s.)* sayings concerning knowledge:

- O Allah, I ask Thee for beneficial knowledge, acceptable action, and good provision (Said by the Prophet *[a.s.]* after the dawn prayer).

- Acquiring knowledge in company for an hour in the night is better than spending the whole night in prayer.

- He who treads the path in search of knowledge, Allah will make that path easy, leading to Paradise for him and those persons who assemble in one of the houses of Allah (mosques), recite the Book of Allah and learn and teach the Qur'an (among themselves). There will descend upon them tranquillity, mercy will cover them, the angels will surround them and Allah will mention them in the presence of those near Him.

- He whom death overtakes while he is engaged in acquiring knowledge with a view to reviving Islam with the help of it, there will be one degree between him and the Prophets in Paradise.

- The man of knowledge increases in submission to Allah, and as for the man of the world, he becomes headstrong and defiant.

- He who issues forth in search of knowledge is busy in the cause of Allah until he returns from his quest.

- Allah, His angels and all those in Heaven and on Earth,

---

[4] *Recite: In the name of your Lord who creates, creates man from a clot. Recite: And your Lord is the Most Bounteous, Who teaches by the pen, teaches man that which he knew not.* (96:1-5)

even the ants in their hills and the fish in the water, call down blessings on those who instruct people in beneficial knowledge.

- If anyone travels on a road in search of knowledge, Allah will cause him to travel on one of the roads of Paradise. The angels will lower their wings in their great pleasure with one who seeks knowledge, the inhabitants of the heavens and the Earth and the fish in the deep waters will ask forgiveness for the learned man. The superiority of the learned man over the devout is like that of the moon, on the night when it is full, over the rest of the stars. The learned are the heirs of the Prophets, and the Prophets leave neither *dinar* nor *dirham*, leaving only knowledge, and he who takes it takes an abundant portion.[5]

A very well-known hadith is the Prophet's *(a.s.)* declaration: "The seeking of knowledge is obligatory for every Muslim." The implications of this statement are enormous. The concept of a mysterious and unfathomable God is usurped by the notion of a Supreme Being who encourages the probings of the human intellect, fueled by hearts which hunger for the truth, male and female alike. It is a confirmation of the Sufi viewpoint on the reason for Allah's creating the universe and humankind within it, i.e., Allah's wish to be known.

All of the prophets attained high degrees of virtuous traits commensurate with the needs of their people. As Allah revealed more of His wisdom, those who carried the news received an increased capacity to bear it, because the knowledge they transmitted was designed to be reflected in their living example. The station of prophethood reached maturity in Muhammad *(a.s.)*. The spiritual and social cohesion brought about through his work provided favorable circumstances for the keeping of permanent,

---

[5] *Dinar* and *dirham*: Arabic monetary units.

unadulterated records. Therefore, the latest Scripture bestowed upon mankind, the Holy Quran, was duly recorded and compiled. Unlike the earlier Scriptures, the Quran has never been altered since it issued forth from the mouth of Muhammad *(a.s.)*. The perfect rendering of Allah's knowledge in the Quran finds its living correspondent in the last Prophet *(a.s.)*, who exemplifies the ideal inner and outer reality of the human being. Muhammad *(a.s.)* fully actualizes the outer form and the inner content of the knowledge of Himself which Allah chose to impart to man. All of the virtuous traits which Allah encourages humans to strive to attain are contained within his being. In other words, Muhammad *(a.s.)* is the Quran. His reality is the synthesis of *Ilm-al-Yaqin, Ayn-al-Yaqin,* and *Haqq-al-Yaqin,* the complete scope of Allah's greatest favor to us, which is insight into the ultimate truth.

This day have I perfected your religion for you, completed My favour upon you, and have chosen for you Islam as your religion.
(5:3)

In Muhammad *(a.s.)*, the circle of human development is completed. From His face, His essence, Allah created the Light of Muhammad, which is the spiritual essence of all believers. Allah reinforced the earthly manifestation of His light continuously throughout the history of mankind by sending a succession of prophets to help secure the truth within the hearts of believers. The light-circuit was clinched with the arrival of Muhammad *(a.s.)* in physical form on the earth, as he was the material manifestation of the primordial energy with which Allah chose to grace the human being. Muhammad *(a.s.)* exemplifies the spiritual knowledge and demeanor of *insan-i-kamil.*

He is both the prototype and the ultimate actualization of the human model which Allah had in mind at the outset of creation. The world did not come to an end when Muhammad *(a.s.)* passed away. Civilizations have continued to flourish, wane, and restructure since that time. The human struggle to survive and prosper persists as always, fostered at times by wisdom and justice, at times by ignorance and greed. Scientific progress, with man's subsequent increased capacity to wield power in his universe, calls for a commensurate enlargement of spiritual awareness in order to maintain healthy, balanced societies. Therefore, divine guidance is necessary as long as humans inhabit the earth. This guidance, having been perfected in Muhammad *(a.s.)* and preserved intact in the Holy Quran, is available to all in this sweeping age of communication. The message of the last Prophet *(a.s.)* continues to circulate throughout the globe.

Verily in the messenger of Allah you have a good example for him who looks forward to Allah and the Last Day, and makes zikr of Allah much. (33:21)

Muhammad's *(a.s.)* position as both Universal Prophet and the last of all of the prophets relates to the enhancement of the human being in the broad sense of our common spirituality. By following Allah's advice to emulate his exemplary behavior, human beings hope to attain a state of being which is pleasing to Allah.

For those who wish to plunge deeper into a state of oneness with the essence of Allah, Muhammad's *(a.s.)* designation as *Habibullah*, Allah's beloved, is key. This appellation indicates his uniquely intimate relationship with the Creator, a flowering of the divine essence within the heart of man. The method of inner spiritual development which leads to such a state was privately taught by Muhammad *(a.s.)* to two of his designated successors, Abu Bakr Siddiq (the Truthful) *(r.a.)* and Ali Waliullah (Friend of Allah) *(r.a.)*. This technique, called *tasawwuf,* has been passed directly through the generations to the present day. The authorized guides of this path based on *zikr,* remembrance of Allah, are the Sufi *shaykhs.* These teachers are the inheritors of Prophet Muhammad *(a.s.)* in their inner spiritual states, in their outward comportment, and in their role as guides and protectors within their communities. Through them, Allah continues to disseminate His message of light and love. The divine knowledge transmitted by each of His prophets is thus sustained, and the ancient covenant between God and man is preserved intact.

5. Initiation into *Tariqa*

Bismillah er Rahman er Rahim

*Verily those who pledge their allegiance to you (Muhammad),
pledge allegiance only to Allah. The Hand of Allah is over their
hands. So whoever breaks his oath, breaks it only to his own nafs'
harm, and whoever keeps his covenant with Allah, on him will
He soon bestow a great reward.* (48:10)

While Allah has never mandated more than belief in His
sovereignty and righteous conduct based on His moral codes,
there have invariably existed certain individuals for whom simple compliance with such codes has not satisfied their deeper
spiritual yearnings. These are the people of whom Allah said, "I
have created some people for my *zat*," which is the divine
essence. Their spiritual gratification comes only with the attain-
ment of a state of oneness with their Lord while living in the
flesh on earth. This high spiritual station was held by many
prophets and other saintly individuals, and was handed down in
turn to a few of their followers who wished for this profound
state. In the Jewish tradition, the Kabbala was a method through
which this was achieved by some. Within Islam, the means
through which the seeker aspires to unity with Allah is the way
of *tasawwuf*, known in the West as Sufism.

The Sufi path is modeled on the *miraj*, Prophet

Muhammad's *(a.s.)* night journey to the presence of Allah while still living on earth. He returned with experiential knowledge which could lead his devout followers to their own personal annihilation in the divine essence. The first of his companions to ask about the lessons learned during the *miraj* was Muhammad's *(a.s.)* cousin Ali *(r.a.)*. The following account of a conversation between the Prophet *(a.s.)* and Ali *(r.a.)*, which highlights two key elements of the path of *tasawwuf,* is transmitted by the great Sufi saint Shaykh *Gawsul Azam*[1] Abdul Qadir Geylani *(r.a.)* in his book of Sufi teachings, *Language of Gems,* written in the twelfth century:

> In the Hadiths it is said that the Prophet *(a.s.)* took a word from his *sahabe* that they were going to obey Allah.[2] Thus taking one's word, i.e., making a pact *(biat),* is modeled after such occasions, and is what makes it legal. Ali *(r.a.)* asked the Messenger of Allah *(a.s.),*
>
> "Which is the easiest and the most revered path in the presence of Allah, for those servants who wish to be close to Allah?"
>
> "O Ali, you must continue making *zikr* of Allah in private."[3]
>
> "So, the merit of *zikr* is this high! But everything is making *zikr* of Allah!"
>
> Upon this the Prophet said, "Don't get carried away, Ali. Allah is not going to destroy the world as long as there are people who are saying 'Allah'."

---

[1] *Gawsul Azam*: The Supreme Helper; One of the many honorific titles of Shaykh Abdul Qadir Geylani. The founder of the Qadiri school of Sufism, he is one of Islam's greatest saints.

[2] *Sahabe*: companions of the Prophet

[3] *Zikr*: remembrance of Allah, which in Sufism has been developed into a formalized ritual

"O, Messenger of Allah, can you teach me how to make *zikr?*"

"Let me say it three times, and you listen. Then, you say it three times, and I will listen." He closed his eyes and raised his voice and said, "*La ilaha illa 'llah*" three times, and Ali listened.

Then Ali *(r.a.)* closed his eyes and raised his voice and said, "*La ilaha illa 'llah*" three times.

This is the origin of inculcating *zikr* in the *murid*. May Allah make us reach this.

Shaykh Abdul Qadir Geylani *(r.a.)* first cites the legal precedent of the pact known as *biat*, which is taken between the Sufi *shaykh* and his student, the *murid* or *dervish*.[4] Because Muhammad *(a.s.)* often took solemn pledges of loyalty from his close companions, it became standard practice for Sufi masters to initiate their students in this way. The terms of *biat* extend to such specifics as the *murid's* earnest intention to follow the *shaykh's* teachings and maintain loyalty to his spiritual ancestors, reciprocated by the *shaykh's* promise to help and guide the *murid* to the best of his ability, and to protect him from spiritual dangers. The above mentioned interaction between the Prophet *(a.s.)* and Ali *(r.a.)* was in fact the first biat, or initiation into the path of *tasawwuf.* As Shaykh Abdul Qadir *(r.a.)* mentions, the gist of this exercise was, and is now, the inculcation of *zikr* into the heart of the initiate. *Zikr*, both in its ritualized sense and a less formal, but constant state of remembrance, is a major means by which a student of Sufism reaches unity with Allah.

---

[4]The terms *murid* and *dervish*, although they have subtle differences in meaning, are often used interchangeably. *Dervish* connotes a degree of spiritual maturity not necessarily present in a beginning student.

The First Covenant

*And (remember) when your Lord brought forth from the Children
of Adam, from their loins, their descendents, and made them testify of themselves, (saying): Am I not your Lord? They said: Yes, verily. We testify. (That was) lest you should say at the Day of
Resurrection: Of this we were unaware.* (7:172)

Taking the *shaykh's* hand in *biat* is fundamentally a reenact-
ment of the primordial covenant made between Allah and the
souls following their creation. Allah created the souls of human
beings in the world of spirit before He sent them to earth to be
clothed in material bodies. The first created entity to be separated from Allah's essential energy was the soul-light of Muhammad
(a.s.), from which all human souls were then spun out. This is
the basis for the Biblical statement that man was created in God's
image. Allah's intention in creating human beings was to be
known as the eternally existing Reality and the Creator of the
universe. The ultimate result of man's divinely ordained search
for knowledge of the universe, and of himself, is the realization
that he is indeed fashioned from Allah's own substance, that his
spiritual homeland is the essence of Allah.

The Creator knew that as man consorted with the physical
trappings of earthly existence, he would be inclined to forget his
higher nature and purpose in life. As a reminder to the souls of
their divine origin, along with their differentiated status as created
beings, Allah forged the first sacred covenant in the realm of spirit. This primordial accord was enacted between God and man
when He asked us, *Am I not your Lord?* Our answer in the affir-
mative sealed the original human pact with the Creator.

In His mercy, Allah did not simply abandon mankind to the

distractions of the flesh after the souls had been sent into their bodies. As the need arose He sent prophets with messages of divine wisdom and scriptures as stores of knowledge bequeathed to mankind for posterity. The divine covenants, which were renewed periodically with the prophets throughout man's earthly saga, were in essence predicated on the prior agreement in the spiritual world, the accord that had been wrought at the outset of our existence.

Tariqa: The Path of the Prophet

And that those who have been given knowledge may know that this is the truth from your Lord, so that they may believe therein and their hearts may submit humbly to Him. For Allah verily is the Guide of those who believe to the Straight Way. (22:54)

The guidance subsumed within each of the divine covenants pertains to the actions of man in the world. As in the Ten Commandments, which were mandated as part of the covenant between God and the community of Prophet Musa *(a.s.)*, the objective was to supply man with directives for righteous behavior. Such conduct would promote a harmonious milieu for man, well-integrated within the universal schema of spiritual and physical laws. In Islam, the compilation of ordinances concerning appropriate behavior for human beings is known as *sharia*. The regulations which comprise *sharia* are based on Quranic injunctions and traditional accounts of Prophet Muhammad's *(a.s.)* sayings as recorded in the *hadiths*. As with the covenants of older history and the canonical laws derived therefrom, the domain of *sharia* is the outer man, i.e., how he should act in order to maximize his true potential and please his Creator.

The believer who yearns for something deeper than the promised reward of eternal salvation for good behavior is faced with a challenge which springs from within. Happiness for him is not achieved by clinging to the hope of endless delights in Paradise, nor is he motivated toward being good in order to avoid the agonies of hell. Consciously or unconsciously, this seeker is after absolute truth. It is the inner man who remembers when he was not separated from his Lord, and now longs to be reunited with his true Beloved. Although in fact no real dichotomy exists, the mind learned to create a separate entity of itself, wrapped up in human flesh, when the self was born. This seeker craves for the conscious realization of what his heart already knows—that he is connected very intimately with the essence of Allah, and in fact his true nature lies in the experience of knowing that ultimate reality. The task at hand thus becomes to discover where his "self" fits in relation to Allah's unlimited Being.

In order for the seeker to find his way through his material self and pass to the formless essence within, he must step from *sharia* into *tariqa*, which is the bridge between the outer and inner human being. For Sufis, *sharia* is what the Prophet *(a.s.)* said, and *tariqa* is what the Prophet *(a.s.)* did. It is the path he took which brought him to the presence of Allah. The method of *tasawwuf* is a compilation of practices designed to open the path and guide the student through the pitfalls he may encounter thereon.

In the inner world, the realm of spirit, new dimensions of experience may be revealed, as the familiar, rational structure of one's world seems to give way to illogical or nonsensical occurrences such as seeing spiritual beings or receiving internal messages. Such phenomena can be quite disconcerting to a sober individual who is new to the path. The Sufi *murid's* disquiet is, however, allayed considerably as he learns that there exists an entire hierarchy of spiritual beings at the ready, whose sole intent is to help ease his way through the unusual territory of *tariqa*. During his progression through *tariqa*, what seemed at one time fantastic he may later accept as a normal occurrence within the range of his everyday experience. As the *murid* becomes open to the unseen realm, he realizes that the created world exists along a continuum from the material to the ethereal. Just as he is learning that he is comprised of an inner and outer self, so he discovers that this principle abides in the cosmos at large.

6. The Spiritual Administration

Bismillah er Rahman er Rahim

He has the Power over His slaves. He sends guardians over you until, when death comes to one of you, Our messengers receive him, and they never fail in their duty. (6:61)

In his walk through *tariqa*, the Sufi *murid* observes that no rigid line separates the material world from the unseen. As his inner organs of perception open, so does his universe. He may soon discover that the seemingly expanded world is peopled by a class of helpers known as *awliya*, or *walis*.[1] These saintly ones have reached a high state of surrender to the Creator. For their earnest dedication, Allah has bestowed on them His name *Al-Wali*, the Protecting Friend. They are the means through which Allah activates His attribute of protective friendship. The many grades of *wilayat*, or *wali*hood, are based on levels of spiritual advancement, and there are several categories of *walis* based on specific job assignments.

Allah acts through *walis* in specifically designated ways, allowing them to exercise His protective and/or creative powers. For example, some are spiritual healers, whose ability may either be specific to certain illnesses, or may serve to treat any sickness.

---

[1] *Awliya*: Plural form of *wali*. For ease of reading, the author will frequently use the English pluralization suffix "s" throughout this book, rather than the original, and strictly proper, Arabic pluralization of terms.

There are *walis* who have been appointed to spiritually protect animals or children, *walis* assigned to manage societal affairs, *walis* who have been given the power to affect weather patterns, *walis* whose sole purpose is to act as living prisms for Allah's light. Depending on the need, a particular *wali* may be assigned to multiple jobs. Many *walis* who have passed away into the spiritual realm continue to work in this world from their spiritual dimension.

Although some *walis* may be recognized as such, others work covertly, obeying Allah's commands in a clandestine fashion. Hidden *walis*, who may assume a variety of tasks, are known as *abdal*. Although they do not represent Sufism outwardly, as *shaykhs* do, they work in the material world, albeit concealed. The *abdal* live in a state of continuous self-annihilation, so that they may carry out Allah's commands spontaneously, without the need of a messenger from the outside or even from within themselves in the form of revelation.

The *abdal* are the deputies of the *qutb*, the *wali* who is the primary living receptacle of Allah's spiritual energy. The *qutb* is the chief spiritual administrator of the outer world, through whom passes Allah's dynamic power, which is constantly reshaping His earthly creation. The *qutb*'s will has become synonymous with Allah's own in his state of annihilation, and it is through him that the *shaykhs* receive their spiritual energy. According to the needs of the time, there may be more than one *qutb* assigned to separate areas of the globe, or there may be one supreme *qutb* of the time. All are answerable to spiritual superiors in the inner, or unseen, realm. Partly because of the highly sensitive nature of the *qutb*'s job, his identity is veiled to the world. Nor is there need for disclosure, as he works mainly as an agent to filter Allah's energy throughout the world from its source in the unseen. Rather than being a messenger of Allah's light, he is a conduit.

The *walis* who have been assigned to teach *tasawwuf* in the world, the messengers of Allah's light, are known as *shaykhs*. They work visibly in the world, and base their guidance on directives which issue from supervisors in the unseen realm. Those *shaykhs* who are responsible for the training of other *shaykhs* are called *murshids*. The senior living *shaykhs* of the respective schools of Sufism are *murshids*, and are responsible for the hands-on regulation of *tasawwuf*.

The roles of *qutb*, *murshid*, *shaykh*, and *badal*[2] are not necessarily mutually exclusive. For example, a *shaykh* may also be a *murshid*, while simultaneously designated as a *qutb*. The distinction lies in the respective functions performed by the holder/s of such titles. Together they comprise the administration of *tasawwuf* in the seen, material, world.

The *Silsila*

And hold fast, all together, to the rope which Allah (stretches out for you), and do not separate. And remember with gratitude Allah's favor on you; for you were enemies and He joined your hearts in love, so that by His grace, you became brothers; and you were on the brink of a pit of fire, and He saved you from it. Thus does Allah make His signs clear to you, that you may be guided.
(3:103)

The upper echelon of the administration of *tasawwuf* holds court in the unseen world. Under the direction of Prophet Muhammad *(a.s.)* and his commanding council, many *walis*

---

[2]*Badal*: Singular form of *abdal*.

who have passed away continue to work from their posts in the spiritual realm, having been functionaries of *tasawwuf* during their lives on earth.

Every true *shaykh* has been appointed to the task of teaching *tasawwuf* by his own *shaykh*, who was previously assigned by his *shaykh*, and so on, in a line which stretches back to the Prophet *(a.s.)*. Each of the several schools, or *tariqas*, of Sufism, is thus supported by its own ancestral lineage of spiritual teachers, called *silsila*. Every *silsila* is documented in writing, and each line of descent, though distinct, proceeds from the authoritative decree of Prophet Muhammad *(a.s.)*. In the act of taking *biat*, the *murid* makes spiritual connection not only with his own *shaykh*, but with the entire chain of *shaykhs* within the Sufi order to which his *shaykh* belongs. In taking hand with all of his *shaykh*'s spiritual ancestors, the *murid* makes a bond ultimately with the Prophet *(a.s.)* himself. This connecting with his *silsila* is what Sufis regard as "holding onto the rope" of Allah.

Through Allah's name *Al-Hayy*, the Living, the preceding *shaykhs* continue to inspire and guide the living *shaykhs*, who are their earthly representatives. Even after their physical death, the teachers of the path to Allah maintain their holy assignment, as long as they have students to teach. The students of *tasawwuf* are exceptionally favored by this generous help from the unseen realm.

The Executive Committee

The Sufi *shaykh* understands his profound indebtedness to his superiors in the chain of command which comprises his *silsila*. These *pirs* and *shaykhs* are the managing directors of the Sufi path,[3] under the leadership of Prophet Muhammad *(a.s.)*. With

---

[3] *Pir:* Founder or living head of a Sufi *tariqa;* general term for *shaykhs* within a *silsila.*

his executive decision, mature students are given the *ijaza*, or permission to teach as Sufi *shaykhs*, as well as the spiritual power called *tasarruf*, which enables the *shaykh* to help transform willing hearts on the Sufi path. The entire gamut of the study and expression of *tasawwuf* is governed from unseen quarters by Muhammad *(a.s.)*, the seal of the prophets and personification of the perfect human being. His executive committee is comprised of his four *khalifas*[4] Abu Bakr, Umar, Uthman, and Ali *(r.a.)*, as well as the founding *pirs* of each of the Sufi *tariqas*. The members of each *silsila* receive their orders from the executive committee of the Prophet *(a.s.)*, and pass information and directives through the chain in the unseen to the *shaykhs* in the seen. From his post in the visible world, the *qutb* of the time holds the pivotal point in the transmission of spiritual energy from the inner to the outer world.

Prophet Muhammad *(a.s.)*, his *khalifas*, the *pirs* of the *tariqas* and their respective *silsilas*, therefore, comprise the aggregate which functions as the inner administration of *tasawwuf*. The *qutbs*, *abdal*, and *shaykhs* are charged with the execution of their directives, and, as such, comprise the outer spiritual administration.

The Role of *Shaykh*

None will have the power of intercession but him who has made a covenant with his Lord. (19:87)

Allah created human souls according to specific familial hierarchies. Such spiritual kinship predates the incorporation of

---

4 *Khalifa*: Designated representative of the Prophet *(a.s.)* or of a *shaykh*.

the souls into their bodies and may or may not correspond to carnal blood lineages. The founders of each Sufi *tariqa* are close spiritual descendants of Prophet Muhammad *(a.s.)*, and are the patriarchs of their respective spiritual families. For reasons of spiritual ancestry, therefore, the affiliation between a *shaykh* and his *murid* is not circumscribed by the usual teacher-student relationship. The *shaykh* is truly his *murid's* spiritual father.

The *shaykh's* job is to help his *murid* reach the realization of Allah within himself and to protect him from spiritual danger. As *tariqa* is the bridge between the inner and outer worlds, the *shaykh* is the conductor who leads the way across, a living link between outer and inner. He has his feet in both worlds at all times, having been to the other side and sent back, in order to guide his children to their spiritual destination. The *shaykh* is a *wali* who works visibly in the world, while receiving the guidance to carry out this duty from his *pirs* in the unseen. The spiritual energy needed to carry out his duties is sent to him from his *pirs* through the living *qutb*.

The following is a description of a Sufi *shaykh* from *Language of Gems* by Shaykh Abdul Qadir Geylani *(r.a.)*:

> Unless a *shaykh* attains the following twelve virtues in himself, he cannot sit on the *sajjada* (prayer rug) of annihilation and wear the sword of being a helper. Two virtues are from Allah, two are from the Prophet *(a.s.)*, two are from Abu Bakr, two are from Umar, two are from Uthman, and two are from Ali *(r.a.)*.
>
> The ones from Allah are: *sattar* (covering of shame or shortcomings), and *ghaffar* (forgiving much).
>
> The ones from the Prophet *(a.s.)* are: *shafiq* (extreme kindness, mercy), and *rafiq* (extreme softness).

The ones from Abu Bakr are: *sadiq* (loyalty), and *mutasaddiq* (much alms giving).

The ones from Umar are: *amri maruf* (strongly enforcing right action), and *nahy-i-munkar* (forbidding ill deeds).

The ones from Uthman are: *mitam* (hospitality), and *musalli* (praying during the night when everyone else is sleeping).

The ones from Ali are: *alim* (knowing), and *shuja* (courage).

If a *shaykh* doesn't have the following five virtues, he will be a *dajjal* (misleader) who will lead the people into ignorance:

• Outwardly, he should know *sharia*.

• Inwardly, he should be researching *haqiqa* (the state of knowledge of the truth).

• He has to serve his guests with a smiling face.

• He must treat the poor kindly, saying nice words to them. This is the praised *shaykh*, who knows *haram* (what is forbidden) and *halal* (what is permitted).

• He knows how to tame his own *nafs* and how to tame the *nafs* of the wayfarers to *haqiqa*.

The person who is going to be a *shaykh* has to know the religious and natural sciences, and the terminology of the Sufi masters. If he doesn't know these, he cannot be a *murshid* (master). Junaid, may Allah be pleased with him, says, "Our knowledge depends on the Book of Allah (Quran) and *sunna* (observed behavior) of the Prophet. The one who doesn't memorize the *hadith* and write it, who doesn't know the great Book and the terminology of the Sufi masters, who doesn't have any knowledge of the religion, is not a person among the ones who do *irshad* (teach enlightenment). As for me, the person who takes the responsibility of training and raising the *murid* must do this for Allah's sake, not for his *nafs* (egoistic self). When he is raising him and inviting him to fight against his *nafs*, he must be kind, caring, and soft, as a father and mother treat their children. First, he should show him the easy ways, and not give him or her a load he cannot carry. After he takes the *murid's* word that he will leave his ill deeds and start praising Allah, he can slowly, step by step, give him heavier assignments."

The person who wants to train himself without a *shaykh* is actually trying to raise a building without a foundation. A person who is not raised by masters and did not get sacred milk from them is like a child left in the middle of the street. If a person doesn't wear the clothing of *taqwa* (avoiding sins, fearing Allah) in the hands of an alert and authoritative master, he will fall into the trap of his *nafs*, and his *nafs* will play with him as it wants, and it will lower him to baseness. On the other hand, the one who holds a strong handle will be able to see the secret of his existence, and he will be submersed into endless favors and pleasures of Allah. The *murid* who follows his *nafs* and who doesn't listen to his *shaykh* is really denying himself his portion in life.

It is incumbent upon the *shaykh* to have refined his behavior to the worthy degree of Prophet Muhammad *(a.s.)* and his *khalifas (r.a.)*, so that he may be an example for the development of outer excellence. Likewise, he must have reached an advanced state of inner development to be an effective guide thereof. In order for him to lead his *murid* to connection with his inner self, the *shaykh* must have traversed this territory himself, as it is otherwise impossible to show the way.

The inner evolution of the *shaykh* has brought him through the four doors of *tasawwuf*: from *sharia*, which is what Muhammad *(a.s.)* said, through *tariqa*, what Muhammad *(a.s.)*

did, through *haqiqa*, the secret of Muhammad *(a.s.)*, to the state of *marifa*, the being of Muhammad *(a.s.)*. These four stations of the path correspond to the four souls within the human being, who is the microcosm of the entire universe. The *shaykh* has been to the very core of being, at one with the essence of Allah, and back again, upon Allah's command through His Prophet Muhammad *(a.s.)* to lead his children to that promised land. He is the point in which all of the pertinent knowledge is gathered, the interface between the seen and the unseen. As he works visibly in the world, he is part of the outer administration of spiritual matters. Through the *shaykh* in his position in *tariqa*, the inner administration of the Prophet *(a.s.)* finds a voice to guide the seekers of truth. The *shaykh* is the mouthpiece of Muhammad *(a.s.)*, who is the Messenger of Allah. The *shaykh* is thus the inheritor of the prophets, the living means by which Allah's covenant endures.

The conditions of a true *shaykh* are the following:

1. He follows the *sharia*.
2. He has a *silsila* and *ijaza* to teach the path.
3. He speaks about what is in the hearts of those in his presence, and answers questions that they have not spoken aloud.
4. When in his presence, people forget their troubles because he takes their load.
5. He praises Allah and not himself.
6. In his presence you are never bored.

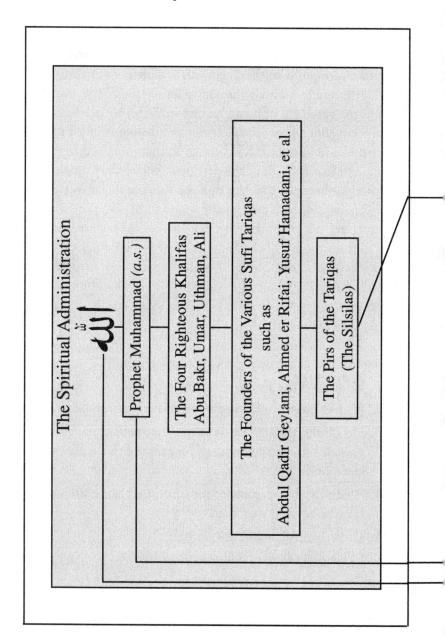

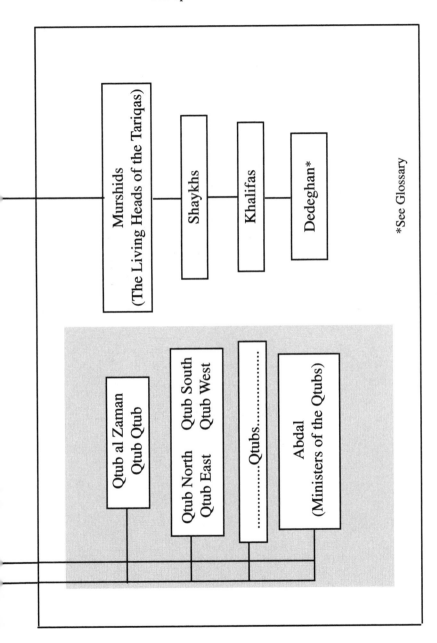

Murshids
(The Living Heads of the Tariqas)

Shaykhs

Khalifas

Dedeghan*

*See Glossary

Qtub al Zaman   Qtub South
Qtub Qtub   Qtub West

Qtub North
Qtub East

.........Qtubs.............

Abdal
(Ministers of the Qtubs)

7. *Tasawwuf*

Bismillah er Rahman er Rahim

And (remember) when We gave Ibrahim the place of the (holy) House, saying: Ascribe no thing as partner to Me, and purify My House for those who make the round (thereof) and those who stand and those who bow and make prostration. (22:26)

The Sufi m*urid*'s quest for unity with Allah takes him through the four doors of *sharia, tariqa, haqiqa,* and *marifa.* This is a journey of conscious connection with the four souls which comprise his spiritual being.[1] *Sharia* pertains to the *jismani ruh,* which is located in the breast. It is the life-force of the material body and its sense-perceptions. *Tariqa* is related to the *seyrani ruh,* which is the link between the outer and inner worlds. The place where *seyrani ruh* and the two deeper souls abide is the heart. *Tasawwuf* is the process through which Allah, through the *shaykh,* clears the path into the depths of the seeker's heart, which is the seat of divine union, and therefore the "house" of God. This course of purification is an inner pilgrimage, the *murid*'s circumambulation of the Kaaba within.

In his twelfth century treatise on Sufism, *Secret of Secrets,* Pir *Gawsul Azam* Abdul Qadir Geylani *(r.a.)* defines the meaning of

---

[1] See Chapter 1, pages 1 & 2.

the word *tasawwuf* as follows:

> The Arabic word *tasawwuf* is spelled by four consonants, *t, s,
> w,* and *f.* The first letter, *t,* symbolizes *tawba,* repentance. This
> first step to be taken on the path has two parts, outer and
> inner. The outer aspect of repentance concerns taking the
> outer perceptions from sins and ill deeds in words and
> actions, and diverting them to obedience. Rebellion should
> be left and submission should be attained. As for the inner
> aspect of repentance, the heart needs to be purified and com-
> plete cooperation needs to be attained, which is different than
> the outer repentance. The second letter, *s,* symbolizes *safa',*
> the state of tranquility. Within this step there are two stages:
> moving towards the purity of the heart and moving towards
> its secret center. The third letter, *w,* symbolizes *wilaya,* saint-
> hood, or protecting friendship. When the truth comes and
> falsehood has vanished from the heart, the level of *wilaya* is
> secured there. The fourth letter, *f,* symbolizes *fana,* which
> means "merging in Allah." It is to dissolve among the divine
> Names and attributes. When mortal attributes are shed,
> Allah's attribute *Al-Ahad* (the Unique) takes its place.

In *tariqa* the spiritual heart, as an inner organ of perception,
is awakened to the *murid's* consciousness. His enlightenment is
a grasping of the reality of Allah within. This is why the Sufi way
is known as "the way of the heart."

The Tools and Practices of *Tasawwuf*

Every human being is equipped with the inner circuitry
which joins him with the divine. Many experience moments of
truth, when the circuits light up and knowledge of the absolute
becomes manifest. These times of heightened awareness often
pass as quickly as they come. The method of *tasawwuf* is

designed to enable the seeker to forge a pure and permanent connection, to gain eternal life while living on this earth.

In the methodology of *tasawwuf* several practices are employed in order to effect its desired goal. Unquestionably, the most important of these is the use of *rabita*, or heart-connection. At the moment of *biat*, a valve is opened in the student's spiritual heart, and a spiritual energy connection is made between him and his *shaykh*, along with the entire *silsila*. Herein lies the importance of *ijaza*, the *shaykh's* permission to teach *tasawwuf*. With *ijaza* comes the key used by the *shaykh* to open his *murid's* connection to the spiritual chain, the "rope of Allah." Hence it can be seen that Sufi lineage is not simply a matter of ancestral tradition; it is the dynamic link to Allah's essence, which is activated at *biat* and continues to operate through the use of *rabita*. The *silsila* as a chain of transmission is the means through which Allah transfers knowledge of Himself to the *murid's* heart. It is the cable used to download information, so to speak, from the source. Making *rabita* is accessing that information.

An essential training tool is to instruct the *murid* in the continual use of *rabita*. He is urged to make a deliberate, thoughtful connection to his heart upon every undertaking in his daily life. At the outset of each activity he is taught to make the mental assumption that it is not he, but his *shaykh* who is performing the action. This practice is designed to help the student leave the notion of self-involvement, which in turn leads to the existential knowledge of the illusory nature of his individual self. The mature student of *tasawwuf* realizes that in making *rabita* to his *shaykh*, he is in truth making rabita to Allah.

Utilizing *rabita* is exercising the central tenet and true meaning of Islam, which is surrender. Through continual use of *rabita*, the *murid's* sense of self dissolves in his *shaykh*, the state known as *fanaful shaykh*, then in his *pirs*, as *fanaful pir*, then in the Prophet *(a.s.)*, as *fanaful Rasul*, and, ultimately, in Allah, as *fanafullah*. This is the true state of self-annihilation, more aptly conceived of as "merging in Allah." When the *murid* comes to the indisputable realization that he truly does not exist, he understands the real truth of "*La ilaha illa 'llah*," that Allah alone exists.

In the relationship between *shaykh* and student lies the key to the *murid's* spiritual advancement. The element of love, *Al-Wadud*, has to exist between them. Love is the medium of unity, the process through which the electromagnetic vibrations produced by the heart and mind are working in tandem, thereby setting up the optimum scenario for spiritual learning.[2] *Rabita* cannot produce the desired effect if not accompanied by love.

Along with the establishment of connection with the *silsila*, during the initiation process into *tariqa* the *shaykh* employs a technique known as *talqin*, inculcation. The practice of *talqin* is the directed use of the mind to plant the seeds of positive change in the *murid's* heart. Through *talqin*, the heart of the *murid* is instilled with *zikr* through the invocation of several of His Beautiful Names. Other ritual prayers are also implanted in the *murid's* heart during *biat*. Throughout the *murid's* training, the *shaykh* is in constant *rabita* with him, and uses *talqin* regularly to help his student, often from afar.

Shaytan (Satan) also likes to use *talqin* for the opposite purpose. His wish is to lead people away from Allah, especially those who seem likely to actually succeed in approaching inti-

---

[2] "... the heart produces by far the strongest electromagnetic signal—a signal that is broadcast to all the other cells of the body...we know that between the heart and the brain there exist neurological connections plus a more recently discovered direct neurochemical and electrochemical link." William C. Gough "The Cellular Communication Process and Alternative Modes of Healing" (San Rafael, CA, 1998), p.12.

macy with the Creator.[3] However, Allah decreed to Shaytan:

As for My (faithful) servants—Over them you have no power, and your Lord is enough as (their) Trustee. (17: 65)

The *shaykh's* job is to protect his *murid* from spiritual danger by utilizing *talqin*, both to fix Allah's light in the *murid's* heart and to work against any counterproductive effort made by Shaytan. The *murid* is likewise instructed in the use of this mechanism for self-regulatory purposes, whereby he can make an effort to distance himself from negative attributes. Through the willful mental conditioning of *talqin*, he intends to convince himself to forego inappropriate thoughts or behavior. His use of *talqin* can also be beneficial in reinforcing the work of other assigned practices of *tasawwuf.*

Recite that which has been inspired in you of the Book, and establish worship. For worship hinders from shameful and unjust deeds, but verily zikr of Allah is greater. And Allah knows what you do.
(29:45)

O you who believe! Make zikr of Allah much.
(33:41)

One of the most treasured practices of the Sufi path is *zikr*, the remembrance of Allah. To be in unity with Allah is to be in a constant state of remembrance of the source of all creation. In the sense that unity is the deepest state of surrender to Allah, this is the true *zikr*, and is the goal of the Sufi path. As a means to

---

3 *Say: I seek refuge in the Lord of mankind, the King of mankind, the God of mankind, From the evil of the sneaking whisperer, Who whispers in the hearts of mankind, Of the jinn and mankind.* (114: 1-6)

achieve that state, *zikr* as a ritualized practice was bequeathed to students of *tasawwuf* by Prophet Muhammad *(a.s.)*.[4]

There are two forms of ceremonial *zikr*: *jahri*, or outward *zikr*, in which one's voice can be heard by others, and *khafi*, or silent *zikr*, in which it can be heard only by oneself. The *jahri* style was taught by the Prophet *(a.s.)* to Hz.[5] Ali *(r.a.)*. The following explanation of the origins of *zikr* is given by Pir Abdul Qadir Geylani in *Secret of Secrets*:

> Hz. Ali *(r.a.)* was the first one to ask our Master the Prophet *(a.s.)* about the path of *zikr*. He asked him to teach him the closest, most precious, and the easiest way. Upon this, Our Master the Prophet *(a.s.)* waited for the angel Jibril *(a.s.)* to come. Jibril *(a.s.)* came and he inculcated *"La ilaha illa 'llah"* into the Prophet *(a.s.)* three times. Our Prophet *(a.s.)* repeated this the same way and then taught it to Ali *(r.a.)*.

(This lamp is found) in houses which Allah has allowed to be exalted and that His Name will be remembered therein. In them He is praised in the mornings and evenings. (24:36)

The ritual ceremony of *zikr* is traditionally held in a Sufi gathering-place known as the *dergah*[6]. In this setting the members of a Sufi *tariqa* together intone certain Names of Allah, thereby invoking the characteristics represented by those Names into the hearts of the congregation. There is a traditional order in which Allah's Names are mentioned in *zikr*, and each one is repeated several, often hundreds of times in unison by the group.

---

[4] See Chapter 5, pages 43 & 44.

[5] Hz.: *Hazreti* or *Hadrat*, meaning The Honorable; this term is often used preceding the names of the prophets and other spiritually distinguished individuals to denote respect.

[6] *Dergah*: the traditional name of the Sufi gathering place, also known as *tekke* or *khanaqah*.

Certain movements, such as swaying back and forth or turning from right to left, are incorporated into the activity during the intonations, and are likewise performed in unison. In some *tariqas* a prayerful rotation of the whole body, arms extended while pivoting on one foot, is traditional.[7]

Each of the Beautiful Names invoked during *zikr* is a key to a spiritual level within the heart. In the midst of such spiritual concentration, participants sometimes travel to profound dimensions of reality. This refreshment to the soul helps to provide encouragement to the *murid* in his sometimes difficult journey to Allah. The effect of *zikr* in the group is to enable each one present to benefit from the augmentation of spiritual energy that a unified effort achieves. In such an atmosphere of concentrated spiritual energy, it is not uncommon for unseen beings such as angels and *walis* to attend the proceedings, thereby bringing additional blessings from Allah.

The seven heavens and the earth and all that is therein constantly repeat His name, and there is not a thing but constantly repeats His praise; but you understand not their way of praising. Verily, He is ever Soft, Forgiving. (17:44)

Those who have mastered *tasawwuf* have become adept at merging with the entire universe in making *zikr* of Allah. The following is a Sufi story about one such enlightened being:

There was once a *murshid* in Turkey who took his students on a picnic. He told them to gather some flowers. All of the students went around the meadow picking flowers for their *shaykh*, each one searching for the most beautiful specimen.

---

[7] Prayerful rotation, known as "turning" is a traditional *zikr* practice of several orders. It has been stylized by the famous so-called "Whirling Dervishes" of Turkey.

One *dervish* saw a dry stem and brought it to the *murshid*. The other *dervishes* laughed, taunting this student by calling him "*abdal*", which means "fool" in Turkish. The *shaykh* said, "Look, they're calling you '*abdal, abdal*.' What do you say to that?" The *dervish* simply said, "*Eywallah*, I accept that." The *shaykh* asked him, "Why did you bring this dead stem?" He replied, "Well, my *shaykh*, I looked around and saw that all the other flowers were making *zikr*. I couldn't stop them from making *zikr*, but when I saw this dead one not doing anything, I decided to bring it." The *shaykh* turned to the other *dervishes* and said, "You were right to call this student '*abdal*,' because the deeper meaning of this word is 'substitutes for Allah,' and he is one of the real '*abdal*.'" From then on the *dervish* was known as Abdal Osman Efendi.

In a holy *hadith*, the Prophet *(a.s.)* said, "Acquiring knowledge in company for an hour in the night is better than spending the whole night in prayer." Therefore, a very beneficial practice employed by the *shaykh* in *tasawwuf* is *sohbet*, the discussion of spiritual matters. In this Sufi tradition, the *shaykh* sits in a circle with his *murids* and proceeds to give an inspired talk on a pertinent spiritual subject. These words are direct teachings from Allah by way of *Haqq-al-Yaqin* operating in the heart of the *shaykh*.[8] It may be that a message comes via one of the members of the *silsila* to the *shaykh*'s heart, yet it is understood that the form in which it is delivered does not diminish the fact that it is knowledge from Allah. One's attentive presence at *sohbet* may be more important to the *murid*'s spiritual growth than any other tool of *tasawwuf*, with the exception of *rabita*.

During *sohbet* the *shaykh* may teach a lesson by telling a story. Sufi storytelling is a tradition whereby the *shaykh* can elu-

---

[8] See Chapter 3, page 22..

cidate a point in a subtle way. A story may be a vehicle whereby a student can be admonished, for example, without being embarrassed in front of his peers. It is crucial for Sufi *shaykhs* and followers of the path to make painstaking attempts to not break anyone's heart, as this is Allah's seat in the house of the human being. The *shaykh* knows when a heart can withstand a strong reproof, and when a more delicate handling of the matter is necessary. Sufi stories provide one means for such subtlety, while simultaneously opening an avenue for thoughtful reflection, for often the stories pose a conundrum that is not readily understood. In a similar way to a Zen koan, these tales can lead the contemplative student to deeper levels of understanding and enlightenment.[9]

Contemplative meditation is another practice prescribed for the student of *tasawwuf*, by which he hopes to reach the enlightenment of spiritual knowledge. Deep spiritual contemplation is known as *tafakkur*. In *tafakkur*, the *murid* poses a question in his mind, makes *rabita* to his heart (to his *shaykh*, to Allah) and waits for the answer to reveal itself. Along the way, he uses deductive reasoning to help his mind work in conjunction with the heart. The mind asks the question, the heart answers, and the mind acts as interpreter, bringing the solution to the forefront of consciousness with clarity.

In *Secret of Secrets* Hz. Abdul Qadir Geylani says the following about *tafakkur*:

Whoever contemplates divine knowing, and wishes to attain a complete sense of knowledge about Allah, the Most High, his contemplation equals a thousand years of ritual worship. The real knowledge of knowing is this. By this knowledge I mean the state of unity. The one who knows reaches his

---

[9] Koan: A story with an inherent riddle used as a teaching practice in Zen Buddhism.

Beloved, the one whom he misses, through this. The end of
this state is to fly spiritually to the realm of real closeness.

*And know that your possessions and your children are a test, and
that with Allah is the great reward.* (8:28)

It is essential that the *shaykh* have a personal and continuous
relationship with his student, because at the moment of *biat* the
shaykh places him in a special curriculum, custom-designed to fit
his individual spiritual needs. This is called *suluk*, the *murid's*
own particular road to Allah, which is regularly monitored by his
shaykh. The outer aspect of *suluk* is the totality of the experiences
he will undergo in life, all of which will carry lessons for him to
learn and tests by which he will be tried. For example, it may
happen that he gets stuck in the same troublesome situation
repeatedly. For the *murid*, this should be taken as an indication
that there is some lesson that he hasn't quite grasped. If he
decides to leave the situation rather than change the thing in
himself which gave rise to it, the pattern will repeat itself until
he gets the message and acts upon it. Everything in his world acts
as a mirror to him. He will continue to see himself reflected back
until he learns to get out of the way, at which point he sees the
reality of Allah reflected in all things.

*We have placed all that is on the earth for you as a glittering show
thereof, that We may test you: which of you is best in conduct.*
(18:7)

In *suluk* the *murid* as *salik*, or seeker, learns that everything
in the outer world has its inner aspect. In other words, everything is a sign from, and pointing to, Allah. Though he may
encounter some strange or miraculous occurrences, the *salik*

learns to regard such incidents as normal episodes in his Sufi trek through life. As he becomes more alert in his broadened scope of observation, his life becomes a Sufi story. This expanded mode of perception helps to promote his realizing that the realms of spiritual and material reality are not mutually exclusive.

Who is it that will lend to Allah a goodly loan, so that Allah will multiply it to his credit many times? Allah gives decrease and largess, and to Him you will return. (2:245)

The world is the *dervish*'s classroom. For him, true enlightenment is not something to be achieved by removing himself from society and taking to the mountaintop or the desert. It is in the day-to-day living in the world that he finds his wilderness, where he learns that it is his own self which is the monster that keeps him captive in the desert of ignorance.

For a Sufi, being close to Allah is reaching a state of nothingness, whereby one is a fitting vehicle through which Allah may act as He wills. The point of Sufi training is not to gain in spirituality, but to realize one's nonexistence and thus to better know, praise, and serve the One who exists. Whatever knowledge one receives on the path to Allah is incomplete and useless if it is not brought from the inner arena of knowledge to the outer field of action. Allah's wish is to develop mature human beings, well integrated in the spiritual and material worlds. This is why the Sufi's learning is in the world, and where the fruit of his spiritual attainments is meant to be put to use. Otherwise, his position is as if he had joined an intellectual club—rich in concepts, short on action, and absolutely void of any spiritual advancement. It behooves the Sufi *murid* to make service to Allah in the world his priority.

Because the *shaykh* is Allah's emissary, His treasure house of knowledge for the student's benefit, and His friend and confidant, the intelligent *murid* regards service to his *shaykh* a priority. In serving one's *shaykh*, one is engaging in behavior pleasing to Allah, as the *shaykh* is one of His beloved people whose sole aim is to help his *murid* reach oneness with Allah. In actively loving his *shaykh* the *murid* attracts Allah's love and facilitates his own progress. Serving one's *shaykh* is especially important for development of the habit of intentionally serving Allah elsewhere in the world. Through serving his *shaykh*, the *murid* is serving Allah.

So make zikr of your Lord and devote yourself to him with
complete devotion. (73:8)

The *shaykh* usually assigns the *murid* his own personal *zikr*, known as *wazifa*.[10] This practice is similar to the congregational *zikr* in that the Names of Allah are repeated in a systematic way. Usually, however, the bodily movements are omitted and rapid repetition is allowed. The number of repetitions of each Name is strictly prescribed; each *murid* receives a variation on a basic formula depending on the individual's stage of development. The *murid* practices *rabita* with his *shaykh* very pointedly while reciting his *wazifa*. Under no circumstances should a student discuss his *wazifa* with another *murid*, as this may breed an unhealthy competitiveness. It is a personal formula to help his purification process, which the *shaykh* modifies when he sees that an improvement has been made in the *murid*'s spiritual condition.

---

[10] *Wazifa*: also known as *tasbih*, which are the strung beads used to count Allah's Beautiful Names.

There may be other practices assigned to the student of *tasawwuf*, such as special diets, spiritual retreat (*halvet*), travel, schooling, etc., all of which depend on the nature of the *murid's suluk*. Although certain standard practices are implemented, it is said that there are as many roads to Allah as there are seekers.

In conclusion, *tasawwuf* is the process of purification of the *murid's* heart, administered by the Sufi *shaykh* in the school of *tariqa*. Like a straight road to the top of the mountain, the way of the *suluk* is surely steeper than the many winding paths which may or may not lead to the summit. Because the *salik's* main problem is within, he relies on his objective and experienced guide to lead him away from himself. It is a great blessing to the student of *tasawwuf* to be able to tap into the purposeful energy which flows through his *shaykh* to help him to success.

8. Fighting the Enemy Within

Bismillah er Rahman er Rahim

As for those who struggle in Our cause, We surely guide them to Our paths, For verily Allah is with those who do right. (29:69)

Allah's wish to be known carries with it the implication that the knower is a being other than Himself. At the very conception of the creation of the universe separation ensued. In their potential form within Allah's essence, Allah's Beautiful Names were unified. When the Names became separated out as the elemental building blocks of creation, His essence changed from potential into kinetic energy. At the outset of this differentiation, Allah's attributes became manifested within the category of His beauty and grace, the *Jamal*, or of His might and power, the *Jalal*. Thus, with creation came the manifestation of opposites.

The human being, having been created from Allah's essence, is likewise composed of His Beautiful Names, and bears also the *Jamal* and *Jalal* aspects of Allah. When the human soul was wrapped up in the material enclosure of the human body, the contrasts between Allah and His creature became sharpened. Here was a finite being whose substance contained all of Allah's attributes, thereby endowing him with the capacity to intimately understand the formless Creator. One attribute through which man was endowed with the ability to comprehend reality, in both its finite and infinite aspects, is *Al-Khabir*. The seat of this Name is human consciousness.

> *And He taught Adam all the names, then showed them to the angels, saying: Tell Me the names of these, if you are truthful.*
> (2:31)

Allah uses the principles of opposition and similarity to teach us about Himself. All of the apparent distinctions among Allah's Names, with the ensuing variety of created entities and the debut of good and evil, set the stage for man's acquiring knowledge. Seemingly endless manifestations of Allah's qualities in creation gives us a taste of the magnitude of Allah's being. From the amazing diversity of created species, or the broad spectrum of light and sound wave frequencies, or the staggering numbers of stars and galaxies, we can extrapolate a concept of the infinite grandeur of Allah's being. Allah points the way to His reality by these conceptual tokens in the principle of similarity. This idea takes hold at first in the imagination. Through the work of *tasawwuf*, it is hoped that one's consciousness will eventually expand and merge with the consciousness of the Creator.

> *Behold! In the creation of the heavens and the earth, and the difference of night and day, and the ships which sail upon the sea for the benefit of mankind, and the water which Allah sends down from the sky, thereby giving life to the earth after its death, and dispersing all kinds of beasts therein, and (in) the deployment of the winds, and the clouds obedient to them between heaven and earth: are signs for people who have sense. (2:164)*

Allah's consciousness resides in the *ruh* of the human being, the four souls of the inner man.[1] When this *ruh* became clothed in the material of the human body, the consciousness as self apart from others began to dominate our field of perception. Allah uses the principle of opposition in the arena of self-individuation, where we see the polarization of opposites both outside of ourselves and within. Thus Allah created what is opposite to Him as a means of approach to Him, in the juxtaposition of the finite with the infinite. For example, the logical extension of the awareness of one's limitations, for the believer, is the realization that he is not god. It is the first part of the equation, "*La ilaha illa 'llah.*" The knowledge that one is not god, "*La ilaha...,*" provides him with the impetus for seeking the truth, "*...illa 'llah,*" the absolute, limitless cause of all creation.

It behooves the seeker on the way to comprehending the boundless reality of Allah to identify his finite self as distinct from his eternal essence, and to have a working knowledge of the character of this aspect of his being. This is part of the meaning of the holy *hadith* in which the Prophet *(a.s.)* states, "When you know yourself, you know Allah." When one identifies, and then surpasses, the consciousness of the material self, the perception of one's intimate connection with Allah throughout his being becomes evident.

The Triad

The human being is a walking laboratory designed for the purpose of observing and understanding Allah, who created him from the lowest of the low to the highest of the high, from the coarsest matter to the finest essence. He is at once a limited,

---

[1] *Ruh*: spirit

flesh-bound corpus and a being capable of manifesting all of Allah's Beautiful Names. Man's animal nature, comprised of bodily functions and egoistic desires, is known as the *nafs*.[2] The *nafs* is tied to the material world, and is therefore restricted by the temporary quality of all creation. The perspective from which the *nafs* perceives reality is itself. This self-biased aspect of the human being is part of the triad which describes him more thoroughly. For the purpose of simplification, *nafs* can be thought of as the outer man, *ruh* as the inner man, and *aql*, the composite faculties of rational discrimination and decision-making, as the bridge between the two.

The basic motivation of the *nafs* is survival, self-preservation. This inherent urge to stay alive and reproduce itself colors its behavior. Void of wisdom, the *nafs* is prone to conduct itself on a reactive basis, as higher knowledge is not within the realm of its operation. However, the fact that the human being does possess the other elements of the triad brings a moral factor into how we perceive and are judged. There are some actions animals engage in within their natural habitat, which, if performed in identical fashion by a human being, would be considered wrong or, at least, indelicate. Cows may mate shamelessly in an open field, but for the human being such an act would be considered open fornication. A pack of wild dogs may partake in a frenzy of ripping apart the carcass of their prey, but they are not denounced as greedy or selfish. The same behavior in man would send him to prison or a mental hospital. Although he has an animal nature, man is distinguished from and considered a higher being than an animal because of his rational and spiritual capac-

---

[2] *Nafs:* See Chapter 2, page 17, footnote 3.

ity, even though his actions far too often do not reflect that capacity.

Consciousness, the attribute of Allah's awareness, *Al-Khabir*, abides in the *ruh* of the human being. Combined with *Al-Alim*, the attribute of Allah's knowing, the spirit-driven consciousness finds expression in the discriminating power of *aql*. The human being is informed from the spirit internally through his heart, which transfers information from the realm of *ruh* to the field of *aql* in his brain, where understanding occurs. The *aql* also receives messages from the *nafs*, as in: "I feel hungry. Let me get something to eat," or even: "That really tasted good. I think I'll help myself to the rest of it" (even if that deprives someone else of a share). Though the *nafs* has a legitimate voice in the human makeup, its tendency is to overstep the bounds of necessity for health and happiness. Therefore, there is a system of checks and balances within us. The role of *aql* is to decipher the incoming information from both the *nafs* and the *ruh*, and to make choices based on that data.

For the spiritually undeveloped, the voice of *nafs* commonly prevails over the voice of *ruh*. As man's consciousness increases, the voice of *ruh* becomes stronger and the voice of *nafs* weaker. Likewise, his capacity and responsibility to modify his behavior increases. In *tariqa*, this continual tempering of character is known as surrender. The true human being is one who has surrendered to Allah to the extent that his *nafs* no longer has control over his actions. He has been brought to a position where his consciousness embraces the whole gamut of Allah's attributes, from the *Jalal* to the *Jamal*.

The human being's conscience is the voice of *ruh* making itself heard from his heart. While ethical knowledge can be derived from his having learned and memorized standards of behaviors, he may learn to direct his attention to the wisdom of the heart and bypass much agonizing over difficult choices. For the Sufi, expanding one's consciousness means being able to hear Allah's voice in the heart. Specific directives from Allah are broadcast to that center of his being. The mature human being makes his choices based on the information housed therein, using his *aql* as arbiter.

The Big *Jihad*

And We shall try you until We test those of you who strive hard (for the cause of Allah) and are patient, and We will test your stamina. (47:31)

A person who has reached the ultimate stage of humanness is known as *insan-i-kamil*, the true human being who has realized his potential to manifest all ninety-nine of Allah's Names. Identifying, opposing, and disciplining the *nafs* are the crux of the method designed to develop the *insan-i-kamil*. The Prophet *(a.s.)* referred to the struggle with the *nafs* when he returned from a great battle and said, "We are coming from the small *jihad* and moving to the big *jihad*."[3] He said that man's greatest enemy is under his ribs, meaning the *nafs*. It was Allah's purpose to provide the *nafs* as a means for his creature to prove the sincerity of his wish to attain closeness to his Creator. In the battle to tame the *nafs* the spiritual warrior accrues deeds of merit as he progresses in *suluk*. Because Allah is just, *Al-Adl*, He implemented this means for his servants to demonstrate their earnestness, that He may justly award them for their efforts. Depending on his intention and effort, the scenario of a self-disciplined human

---

[3] *Jihad*: holy war

being could range, for example, from a guy who gets along well with his neighbors to someone in a constant state of love with, and service to, Allah. The business of *tariqa* is to produce the the latter.

The whole process of *tasawwuf* is designed around one cardinal concept—surrender. The student of *tasawwuf* is enjoined to surrender his *nafs* to Allah. Every Sufi practice holds surrender at the core of its *modus operandi*. With each act of surrender, the student chooses Allah over the *nafs* and thus moves closer to Allah. His goal is to be in a complete state of surrender to Allah at all times. In order to do this he must get his *nafs* out of the way, for that is the only obstacle between himself and his Beloved. By taming the *nafs* and thus rendering it into a state of surrender, the *murid* nullifies its negative influences. Taming the *nafs* is polishing the heart from *nafs'* filth.

According to a Sufi saying, "the heart is *sultan* (king)" because that is where Allah makes His presence known in the human being. Purifying the *nafs* allows the heart to reign in the human being. A cleansed *nafs* has attained the proper manners through which it defers to the *sultan*. To submit the *nafs* to Allah in the way of *tasawwuf* is to "die before you die," in Sufi parlance. One's consciousness naturally increases with the purification of the *nafs*, but it is not the Sufi's purpose to achieve great spiritual vision, or to become preoccupied with the marvels of Allah's miraculous creation. As a famous Naqshbandi *shaykh* from Turkey, Hz. Haji Hamza Ramazanoglu, once said, "It is not seeing; it is not being; it is dying before you die," which brings you close to Allah. For the Sufi, this is the true meaning of Islam. To be a single-minded slave of Allah is the greatest possible honor for the believing servant. To be Allah's lover is to realize one's full potential as a human being. To be all this is to become nothing.

To be with Allah in this lifetime is a great motivation for self-sacrifice, but to be with Allah for all eternity is an even more serious stimulus. There is a story which illustrates this point:

> There was a group of soldiers gathered in the field for the noonday meal in Turkey. It happened that this was the month of Ramadan, when most Muslims fast during the daylight hours. Because of the strenuous nature of their daily routine, many of the soldiers did not maintain the fast, but had sympathy for the few who did. One of these soldiers said to his fasting companion, "You should really be commended for making such a sacrifice of fasting under such difficult circumstances." The other soldier replied, "No, on the contrary, it is you who should be complimented, because you are making the biggest sacrifice. I only have to endure this hardship for a short time, whereas you have made a sacrifice for all eternity."

It is very important that the *nafs* be cleansed in this lifetime to ensure happiness in eternity. It is one's deeds on earth which determine our everlasting place in the future, because the actions and desires of the *nafs* make their imprint on man's spirit, his eternal *ruh*. They give a lasting shape to man's soul, so to speak. Consequently, although *nafs* is the temporary being which houses the *ruh*, its effects can be felt permanently. The Sufi's measure of happiness is how close to Allah's essence his spirit will forever remain after the soul has left the body.

There is no compulsion in religion. The right direction is distinct from error. And he who rejects false deities and believes in Allah has grasped a firm handhold which will never break. Allah is Hearer, Knower. (2:256)

The process of fighting the *nafs* is fundamentally a cutting of attachments—to futile desires, to the illusion of false thinking, to negative habitual actions. Very seldom does the *shaykh* issue direct orders, as it is imperative that the *murid* freely choose his mode of behavior, which is optimally derived from the internalization of the *shaykh's* enlightened teachings. There are general techniques used by the *shaykh* to gently prod the *murid* toward improvement, as well as specific ones addressed to each individual student in his *suluk*.

The *shaykh* doggedly tries to help his student become aware of every thought pattern or behavior that chains him to the self-referring perspective from which he operates. He helps his student identify the sometimes subtle machinations of his own self in his daily encounters with other people. At times, lapses in the *murid's* behavior are brought to his awareness by way of a mirroring effect. It is as if his odious character traits are suddenly exaggerated and displayed in the actions of everyone else in his vicinity. One by one, the student is led to see each personal trait which has become a barrier between himself and Allah reflected in the actions of others. It is when the *murid* suddenly wakes up in the realization that it is himself he has been observing in the mirror of others that the effects of *Ayn-al-Yaqin*, learning by observation, have begun to make their mark. Once awareness comes about, change can take place; the enemy is first confronted, then subdued.

The radical business of detaching oneself from the *nafs* requires help from the outside. Since man's greatest enemy is himself, one needs help from other than himself to do this work. The *shaykh* is his *murid's* experienced guide through the sticky terrain of *nafs*. Just as any traveler through unfamiliar territory needs an expert guide to lead him around pitfalls and past blind alleys, the *murid* needs his *shaykh* to take him away from himself. In this role the *shaykh* is the *murid's* greatest ally and his *nafs'* most dedicated enemy.

Separating the Enemy

And We have created above you seven paths, and We are never unmindful of creation. (23:17)

Life in the world can be seen as a long series of creating *nafs*-attachments, as our desires and expectations grow along with us. The Sufi *murid* quickly learns the considerable magnitude of his attachments and the seemingly endless ways he has learned to put his trust in other than Allah. He realizes that he himself is the idol that must be broken in surrendering to the true God.

The *nafs* is a very stubborn idol, prone as it is toward self-preservation. Any attempt at tampering with its long-cherished habits is naturally met with extreme resistance. Therefore, in *tasawwuf* different aspects of the *nafs* are tackled in sequence, starting from the roughest and most obvious, to the more subtle characteristics. The *nafs* is separated into seven levels, in a divide-and-conquer tactic, so that the *murid* can detach himself by degrees from its influence. With each level of cleansing, the *murid* moves another step closer to unity with Allah with the *shaykh*'s permission, as the *shaykh* holds the key to his student's promotion through the levels of *nafs*. Every level bids a specific practice, which the *shaykh* usually changes when he knows that his student is ready to move on.

These practices are like a trusted physician's prescriptions, to be taken at face value and followed wholeheartedly. Great discretion is called for on the part of the *murid*, who keeps his practices to himself, as they are not meant to be the subject of public discussion. Likewise, the *shaykh* does not divulge his *murid*'s practices to others. In fact, it is unlikely that the *shaykh* will reveal even to the *murid* himself his spiritual attainments. The tactful handling of these private matters helps to hinder possible competitive attitudes among *murids*. Withholding information from the *murid* as to his own status deters pride.

Levels of Nafs

Behold! The commanding nafs encourages evil, except when my Lord bestows mercy. (12:53)

1. *Nafs-i-Ammara*: Commanding Nafs
Traits: narcissistic, mechanical, conditioned, non-reflective, impulsive.
Habits: pride, enmity, cruelty, lust, stinginess.

But I swear by the accusing nafs (that this Scripture is true). (75:2)

2. *Nafs-i-Lawwama*: Blaming Nafs
Traits: conscience, capacity for self-observation.
Habits: backbiting, trickery, conceitedness, hypocrisy, self-consciousness, guilt, fearfulness, wishful thinking, intense desire to please others.

And a nafs and Him who gave order to it and inspired it with a sense of what is wrong for it and (what is) right for it. (91:8)

3. *Nafs-i-Mulhama*: Inspired Nafs
Traits: generosity, gratitude, modesty, empathy, ardent desire.
Habits: liberality lacking discrimination, mystical inflation, tendency toward spiritual greed.

O, you nafs at peace! (89:27)

4. *Nafs-i-Mutmaina*: Tranquil Nafs
Traits: dignity, sincerity, courage, compassion, complete loyalty.

Habits: Attachment to spiritual ambition.

Return to your Lord, content (89:28)

5. *Nafs-i-Radziyya*: Satisfied Nafs
   Traits: endurance, resignation, constancy.
   Habits: personal identification with affliction.

for His being pleased with you! (89:28)

6. *Nafs-i-Mardziyya*: Satisfying Nafs
   Traits: knowledge of Allah, sincerity, unbounded faith
      and hope in existential communion.
   Habits: mystical intoxication, lack of sobriety and bal-
      ance.

*This day have I perfected your religion for you, completed My favor to
you, and have chosen for you as your religion Islam.* (5:3)

7. *Nafs-i-Safiyya*: Purified Nafs
   Traits: freedom from duality, acceptance of Allah's will,
      joy of union, freedom from expectation, content-
      ment.
   Habits: None remaining.

*Except him who repents, and believes and does good works; For
those, Allah will change their evil deeds to good deeds. Allah is
Oft-Forgiving, Most Merciful.* (25:70)

As the *murid* moves through the levels of *nafs,* he is learning
ever deeper levels of surrender by detaching himself from the
myriad demands of personal desires. *Tasawwuf* is a process of
constant surrender, through which one puts *nafs* in its proper
place, which is away from the heart, the *sultan* within. If the
murid chooses not to proceed and stops at any level, this

becomes his *maqam*, or permanent station. The *insan-i-kamil* has surrendered to Allah completely, having become complete master over his *nafs*. Detached from himself, he has strengthened his attachment to Allah in body, mind, and soul. Born with the capability of becoming the lowest of creatures, one who is dominated by his *nafs'* selfish inclinations, in defeating the *nafs* he has attained a station higher than the angels. For him the *nafs* has been transformed into an agent of spiritual advancement. By going through these levels, the *murid* makes the *miraj-i-manawi*, the spiritual journey to the Beloved. Thus he meets Allah face to face, becoming merged and annihilated in Him in a state known as *fanafullah*.

Having come to this pure state, the Sufi may proceed further, with Allah's permission:

Degrees of rank from Him, and forgiveness and mercy.
Allah is Oft-Forgiving, Most Merciful. (4:96)

8. *Bakabillah*: being constant in Allah
9. *Safabillah*: being eternally happy with Allah
10. *Sayrifullah*: journeying in Allah
11. *Sayrima'Allah*: journeying with Allah
12. *Tajallay-i-sirr*: knowing the secret of creation
13. *Tajallay-i-sirrul sirr*: knowing the secret of the secret of creation

9. Surrender

Bismillah er Rahman er Rahim

Verily in the messenger of Allah you have a good example for him who looks forward to Allah and the Last Day, and who makes zikr of Allah much. (33:21)

The Sufi wishes to love and be loved by Allah. In *tariqa* he follows in the Prophet's *(a.s.)* footsteps with this single goal in his heart, because he knows Muhammad *(a.s.)* is *Habibullah*, Allah's lover. He understands that the only way to gain Allah's love is through surrender, for in surrender he denies the selfish urgings of his *nafs* in order to secure Allah's good pleasure. Allah created the Prophet *(a.s.)* as the model of a human being in a state of complete surrender to his Lord. His exquisite state embraced the perfect balance of his inner and outer being. The key to this balance was an unswerving focus on Allah in all things. From the firmness of his faith sprouted his impeccably pure intention to serve his Lord lovingly in thought, word, and deed.

That is because Allah never changes the grace He has bestowed on any people until they first change that which is in their nafs, and (that is) because Allah is Hearer, Knower. (8:53)

In the dynamic of their loving relationship, as the Prophet *(a.s.)*

scrutinized the purity of his intention, Allah in turn increased his faith. The Sufi *murid* is encouraged to reenact such a working relationship with Allah, maintaining focus on Allah with the intention to surrender to Him in every way. Intention is the springboard of surrender, the inner aspect which gives meaning to outer deeds. The intention to act in a way pleasing to Allah is the foundation of faith, because in it is the tacit assumption of Allah's complete sovereignty. The acknowledgment "*La ilaha illa 'llah,*" that, in truth, there is no god but Allah, is implicit in the believer's pure intention. The believer who knows that Allah holds all power, as our Prophet *(a.s.)* did, should preface every action by saying, "*Bismillah er Rahman er Rahim,*" "In the name of Allah, the Most Merciful, the Most Compassionate." In saying this with sincerity, the believer states that he is acting in Allah's name, with Allah's power. Saying "*Bismillah er Rahman er Rahim*" is to be in a state of *rabita* with Allah, and is the beginning of surrender.

Nay, but whoever surrenders his whole person to Allah and does good, his reward is with his Lord; on those shall no fear come, neither shall they grieve. (2:112)

As the beginning of surrender is in the pure intention to act in Allah's name, the completion of surrender is in the outer aspect of right action. Right action is propelled from the heart of one who has been cleansed from his *nafs'* interference, and is shaped by his excellent character. In being cleansed through the levels of *nafs,* the *murid* achieves good *ahlak,* or beautiful character. These are the noble traits which adorned Prophet Muhammad *(a.s.),* and helped bring him to closeness with Allah. Good *ahlak* will carry the *murid* through life's circumstances with grace and fortitude because it is the seedbed of righteous conduct. Putting good *ahlak* to use in action is known as the practice of *adab*[1]. It is the outward manifestation of one's inner willingness to accept Allah's decree and to serve his Lord lovingly. The observance of *adab* is basing one's actions on the premise that Allah is the Owner of the universe. Actions performed with *adab* reflect the realization that even though Allah has given us the conscious will to make decisions, we do not exercise this privilege independently but only as executors of Allah's energy and attributes.

It has been said that the whole of Sufism is *adab*. *Adab* is doing the right thing at the right time in the best way possible. It is the way of harmony, acting with deference to the scheme of the whole. The expression of *adab* is shown in courtesy, politeness, a pleasant social demeanor. It is a way of behaving graciously which flows from the foundation of an inner attitude of surrender. There are general principles of *adab* as well as procedures specific to particular situations. By cultivating good *ahlak*, based on the example of our Prophet *(a.s.)*, our *adab* should flow naturally in various environments. Because Allah has designed every entity with unique characteristics, having *adab* when interacting with the rest of creation is being sensitive to the natural proclivities of all beings, and acting accordingly. It is recognizing Allah in everything that exists, and treating all with respect and humility. Having *adab* is surrender in action. It is acting upon the fundamental truth, *"La ilaha illa 'llah."*

---

[1] *Adab*: courteous behavior

The Virtues of the Prophet

*Those who follow the Messenger-Prophet who can neither read nor
write, whom they will find described in their Torah and their
Gospel, He enjoins on them that which is right and forbids them
that which is wrong; He makes lawful for them all good things
and prohibits for them only the bad; and he relieves them of their
burden and the yokes they wore. Then those who believe in him,
honor him, help him, and follow the Light which is sent down
with him: they are the successful.* (7:157)

Allah says in Quran that he sent Muhammad *(a.s.)* as a
mercy to creation.[2] His softness of character drew disciples to his
side, who were enveloped in the magnetism of his loving kindness. He spoke softly and listened well. Prophet Muhammad
(a.s.) was a single-minded slave of Allah, who never lost focus on
his Beloved. His humility and constancy of purpose bespoke a
state of complete surrender to his Lord. His grateful heart fostered an extreme measure of patience, with which he endured
some very trying circumstances and through which he was able
to tolerate both the foibles and the malice of his fellow human
beings. Such a model as this, Allah's beloved, is a great favor
bestowed on those who wish to be close to Allah. Muhammad
(a.s.) displayed hundreds of characteristics, which his followers
should wisely strive to attain and maintain throughout life.

All believers are enjoined to follow Prophet Muhammad's
(a.s.) example because he is the paradigm of good *ahlak* and the
most excellent *adab*. Allah loved His Prophet *(a.s.)* very much,
and Sufis wish for this love above all else. To this end every Sufi

---

[2] *We sent you not except as a mercy for all the worlds.* (21:107)

is encouraged not only to observe and emulate his flawless behavior, but to truly internalize the Prophet's *(a.s.)* refined demeanor. This cannot be accomplished without profound surrender. We must begin the process with the intention to surrender willingly, and Allah, who has all the power, will then help us to realize His love deep within our being. This love is the fruit of surrender, which is the composite of pure intention with good *ahlak*, and is manifest in acting with *adab* at all times.

Surrender is an ongoing practice. Just as there is no end to Allah's infinite grandeur, there can be no limit to our willingness to yield to our Maker. When the Sufi *murid* makes *rabita* with his *shaykh* with the intention of fighting his *nafs* and acting in Allah's name, the channel between him and the Creator opens up in his heart. This line of Allah's life and love widens with each effort made on the part of His servant.

The conscious development of *ahlak* which is pleasing to Allah is instrumental in the *murid's* fight against the *nafs*. The Sufi model, Muhammad *(a.s.)*, carried hundreds of traits which defined his admirable conduct. Every *murid* should make a special endeavor to internalize at least the following virtues of Prophet Muhammad *(a.s.)*:

> avoidance of sins, belief, caring for relatives, consideration for others, contentment, dedication, dependability, forgiveness, generosity, gratitude, helping others, hiding of shame, humility, intercession, justice, love, loyalty mercy, modesty, obedience, patience, peacefulness, perseverance, protection, respect, security, self-control, softness, surrender, tactfulness, tolerance, truthfulness, understanding, wisdom, worship

And We created you, then gave you forms, then told the angels:
Fall prostrate before Adam! And they fell prostrate, all except Iblis
(Shaytan), who was not of those who make prostration. (Allah)
said: What prevented you from prostrating when I ordered you?
(Iblis) said: I am better than him. You created me from fire and
him you created from mud. (Allah) said: Then go down from here!
It is not for you to show pride here, so get out, for you are of the
most degraded! (7:11-13)

Humility and its counterpart, obedience, are essential
human traits and the hallmarks of *adab*. Obeying Allah in all situations is acting with the humble acknowledgment that He is
sovereign. Although Shaytan was given much knowledge by
Allah, his prideful refusal to obey his Creator banished him forever from His favor, and rendered his knowledge useless. Human
beings are exceptionally endowed with knowledge from Allah,
who has favored us with the means for the expansion of our consciousness in the ocean of His reality. Allah expects only one
thing from His servants in return for His gifts, and that is gratitude. It is with a grateful heart that one approaches true closeness to the Creator and becomes His beloved. The gratitude of
the heart takes outward expression in humility, obedience, generosity, and other qualities inherent in the attitude of surrender.
Having *adab* is always giving Allah the benefit of the doubt in
difficult circumstances by exercising patience.

The privilege of being brought to intimacy with the Creator
warrants extreme self-vigilance, a responsibility which is exactly
proportional to the measure of closeness attained. As the Sufi
progresses through higher spiritual stations, his demeanor must
become more soft and refined. He should strive for a sweetness

and softness of character. As the great Shaykh Hz. Muhyiddin
Ansari *(r.a.)* once said, a Sufi should be "like Turkish Delight." [3]

Adab of the Shaykh

And he who believed said: O my people! Follow me. I will lead
you to the way of right conduct. (40:38)

The *shaykh*, as the representative of Prophet Muhammad
(a.s.), assumes several authoritative roles in the *tariqa*. As Allah
enjoins all Muslims to follow the example of the Prophet *(a.s.)*,
Sufis are urged to follow their *shaykh's* example in terms of general comportment. Therefore, the *shaykh's* very visible role calls
for excellence of conduct in every situation. Because he is
answerable to the entire *silsila*, he must follow the strictest of
standards in conformity with *sharia*, *tariqa*, *haqiqa*, and *marifa*.

There are five potential sources of problems of which the
shaykh should always be aware:

   1) fame
   2) money
   3) persons of the opposite sex
   4) alcohol and drugs
   5) vanity, or thinking that the knowledge belongs to him
      and he doesn't need his own *shaykh* anymore

A mature *shaykh* is in a state of constant *rabita* with his *shaykh*,
whether living yet on this earth or not. A mature *shaykh* assumes
that he himself doesn't exist, and that his *shaykh* is working
through him. As long as he is living in his body on earth, the
shaykh is not immune to the temptations of the *nafs*. Well aware
of the dictum, "The higher the climb, the harder the fall," he

---

[3] Turkish Delight is a soft and delicate confection.

must continually strive to maintain his spiritual station, regardless of the heights he has attained.

The *shaykh's* only concern should be the good of his *murids*. He should act towards them with kindness, love, and compassion, as a father with his children. He must care for them and guide them out of concern for them alone, for Allah's sake. At no time may the *shaykh* be engaged in any sexual activity with his *murids*, neither is he permitted to marry a *murid*, for such a relationship would be considered incestuous. A *shaykh* should know who his children are and never try to take another *shaykh's* student. At times a *shaykh* may send his *murid* to another *shaykh* for some specific guidance, but it is improper for the other *shaykh* to initiate this transfer. Likewise, it is bad *adab* for a *murid* of one *shaykh* to seek guidance from another *shaykh* unless he has been formally released as the former *shaykh's* *murid*.

Every Sufi *murid* requires specialized attention from his *shaykh*. The *shaykh* must be available to spend time with all of his students, even if circumstances allow for only a long-distance relationship. Regarding conversations of a personal nature, the *shaykh* must maintain strict confidentiality between himself and his *murid*.

A mature *shaykh* never recruits *murids*. Allah brings the students to him, and permits only the sincere to remain under the *shaykh's* wing. The *shaykh* should only accept those whom his heart recognizes as his own children and he should never glorify himself by broadcasting how many followers he may have. The number of *murids* does not indicate the spiritual position of the *shaykh*. It is the quality of *murids*, how close they have come to Allah, which is important.

Take alms of their wealth, so thereby you may purify them and make them grow, and pray for them. For your prayer is a help to them. Allah is Hearer, Knower. (9:103)

As in any religious organization, Sufi *murids* may be asked for regular tithings or service to their *tariqa* for operational purposes. In no way does this give the *shaykh carte blanche* with his *murid's* finances. All monies must be donated willingly, and the *shaykh* should never resort to extortion or any other opportunistic activity. It is the *shaykh's* right to ask for payment for expenses such as running the *dergah* and community meals, just as he may rightfully expect his *murids* to shoulder his traveling expenses when they invite him for out-of-town engagements. If any *murid* wishes to make additional donations to the *shaykh* for the upkeep of his family, this is acceptable. In an optimum situation, the Sufi congregation would provide their clergyman, the *shaykh*, with a yearly salary for his services.

The Messenger believes in what has been revealed to him from his Lord, as do the believers. Each one believes in Allah, His angels, His books, and His messengers. "We make no distinction among any of His messengers." And they say: "We hear, and we obey: (We seek) Your forgiveness, our Lord, and to You is the journeying." (2:285)

With the general public, a *shaykh* must act as the representative of Prophet Muhammad *(a.s.)*, with kindness and tolerance. His interactions with people should be on the level of their understanding. With his *murids*, the *shaykh* assumes the role of father. When in the presence of another *shaykh*, he should always treat him as his equal or better. It is Allah's business to know who of His servants merits closeness to Him, and He bestows His love on whomever He wishes. A mature *shaykh* recognizes this fact and never conceitedly tries to assume authority over another *shaykh*, but modestly acknowledges their brotherhood and singularity of purpose. He knows that it is Allah who deserves the praise at all times.

Adab with the Shaykh

O You who believe! Enter not the dwellings of the Prophet for a meal without waiting for the proper time, unless permission be granted you. But if you are invited, enter, and, when your meal is ended, then disperse. Linger not for conversation. For that would cause annoyance to the Prophet, and he would be timid about (asking) you (to go); but Allah is not timid about the truth. And when you ask of them (the wives of the Prophet) anything, ask it of them from behind a veil. That is purer for your hearts and for their hearts. And it is not for you to cause annoyance to the Messenger of Allah, nor that you should ever marry his wives after him. Truly that in Allah's sight would be an enormity. (33:53)

The *murid* who is new to the path should understand that observing proper *adab* is a central practice for his spiritual advancement, helping to balance his inner state with his outer being. The *shaykh* is the *murid's* door to Allah, and therefore strict standards should be observed in his behavior with his teacher. In practicing good *adab* with his *shaykh*, the student is preparing for the meeting with his Lord. Because Allah does not tolerate mistreatment of His friends' hearts, the worst thing a *murid* can do is to break his *shaykh's* heart.

While in the presence of his *shaykh*, the *murid's* attitude should be attentive and oriented toward service. While his *shaykh* is speaking, he should be quiet and listen with an open heart, as this is Allah's lesson for him. If he does not understand or disagrees with a statement made by his *shaykh*, he should never summarily dismiss it. Rather, it should be stored in his mental data bank, as the meaning may become clear at some time in the future. Thus adjures the motto: "Even if your *shaykh* is wrong, he's right." The *murid* is wise to regard any lesson directed to someone else in the circle as his own. It may be the case that the *shaykh* is trying to save the *murid* from a breach of *adab* or that he is being very careful not to hurt his feelings by apparently directing a lesson to someone other than the main intended recipient.

The *murid* should always assume an attitude of respect within the hierarchical structure of the *tariqa*. Just as in any social organization, there are avenues of access to information. The *shaykh*'s representative managers are his designated *khalifas*. Questions of *adab* or logistical issues of a social nature, for example, making appointments with the *shaykh* or finding directions to the center, should always be addressed to a *khalifa* or senior member of the *tariqa*. The new *murid* is wise to ask the *khalifa* about *adab* in the *dergah* or the proper etiquette to be observed when visiting the *shaykh* at his home, as these are situations in which an extra measure of respect is reflected in requisite procedures. It is helpful for him to remember that the *shaykh* represents the Prophet *(a.s.)*, and that he and his family should be treated accordingly.[4] It behooves the student to make regular contact with his *shaykh*, and he should do so, out of simple courtesy, at appropriate hours.

---

[4] For more specific information on *adab*, see the journal/newsletter of the Qadiri Rifai Tariqa, *Call of the Divine*, Vol. 2, nos. 1-4 and Vol. 3, nos. 1, 2.

Nay, but Allah must you serve, and be of those who give thanks!
(39:66)

Allah knows that human beings are quite prone to making mistakes, and is most forgiving and merciful, for the *murid's* sincere intention is always noted. The *murid* should understand, however, that his expression of gratitude is at the core of *adab*. Gratitude is expressed in three ways: thankfulness of the heart, thankfulness of the tongue, and thankfulness of action. The latter is the easiest for human beings to overlook, but the effort entailed in the action of gratitude carries major blessings to the thankful one. When the *shaykh* has performed some specific service, such as a spiritual healing or intensive counseling session, its benefits are sustained by reciprocation, because Allah increases the blessings of those who are thankful. A donation of money or work-service to the *tariqa* are practical ways in which one can demonstrate his gratitude for services rendered by the *shaykh* for Allah's sake.

10. Other Beings

Bismillah er Rahman er Rahim

And He taught Adam all the names, then showed them to the angels, saying: Tell Me the names of these, if you are truthful. (2:31)

Allah does not obligate human beings to assume a blind belief in His existence. Because His purpose was to create the human as His deputy on earth, Allah provided him with the knowledge essential for that position. Without that knowledge it is impossible for man to assume the role of Allah's representative. To be fully human is to be apprised of the basic dynamics upon which the universe was created, to embrace that knowledge, and to act in accordance with it. Accepting the knowledge which Allah bestowed on mankind is the kernel of belief. Because only Allah has the capacity to comprehend His limitless reality, the conditions upon which He accepts the validity of belief in human beings are specific: belief in Allah, His scriptures, His messengers and prophets, His angels, the Judgment Day, and that Allah has indisputable and overriding power in creation.

Praise be to Allah, Lord of the Worlds! (1:1)

With a purpose to create His vicegerent on earth, Allah fashioned the nature of humans to span the extremes of creation. A living composite of the coarsest material with the finest awareness, man, of all creatures, enjoys the broadest scope of understanding Allah's reality. He is the pilot of a mass of cooperating and competing chemical processes, and employs Allah's bequest of discrimination and free will to complete his intimate consciousness of the Creator.

The human being's potential breadth of experience does not, however, preclude the existence of other intelligent or self-conscious beings in the universe. There may be many worlds inhabited by such beings, known in Sufi tradition as the *ehli samawat*, people of the heavens. Ancient mythology and literature, including the Bible and other scriptures, make frequent mention of godlike beings and angelic creatures. Because the Sufi's primary concern is his own struggle to cultivate a loving relationship with Allah, in *tariqa* there is small effort devoted to the lives and habits of nonhuman beings. However, there are two types of beings with whom humans have interacted continually throughout history and who therefore warrant brief study: the angels and the jinn.

In our universe two distinct genres of spiritual administration exist. One is Allah's "personal" corps of angels, created for the sole purpose of carrying out His will directly. The other is the spiritual administration of Allah's vicegerent on earth, the human being, together with that of the jinn, presided over by Prophet Muhammad *(a.s.)*.

The Angels

Almost might the heavens above be rent asunder while the angels hymn the praise of their Lord and ask forgiveness for those on the earth. Behold! Allah, He is the Forgiver, the Merciful. (42:5)

Angels are beings of light, created, as are all believers, from the *Nur-i-Muhammad*, the Light of Muhammad. Some angels have been living since the beginning of creation, while others are relative newcomers to the universal community. Allah continuously creates angels by the light of His Beautiful Names when human beings praise their Lord and mention His Names and when blessings are sent upon the Prophet *(a.s.)*. Angels are the means by which Allah directly produces dynamic events in creation. When Allah in His pure essence intends a thing to happen, they carry out His wishes throughout the universe of His manifestation. Although they have consciousness of self as individual beings, angels' capabilities include no possibility to act in opposition to their Lord. Their perfectly loyal nature, replete with characteristics proper to their function as Allah's unflagging servants and helpers, prevents them from sin or disobedience to the Creator.

The Arabic term for angel, *malak*, means "able to do," and aptly describes their ability to provide service to the Creator in a variety of ways. Allah created one class of angels in the *alam-i-jabbarut*, the second created realm. These are the archangels, who have a wide range of powers. Although there may exist many thousands of archangels, in Islamic tradition four are especially mentioned. Jibril *(a.s.)* is the archangel charged with revealing Allah's truth to the prophets. He is the messenger who revealed the Quran to Prophet Muhammad *(a.s.)* in person after the Prophet *(a.s.)* had received the inspiration from Allah internally. Allah adjured Muhammad *(a.s.)* to wait for outer confirmation of His revelation from Jibril *(a.s.)* before he announced a new message, because He knew of the propensity of the wayward devil to subtly deliver false information.[1] Among the tasks of rev-

---

[1] *Then exalted be Allah, the True King! And hasten not (O Muhammad) with the Qur'an before its revelation has been perfected for you and say: My Lord! Increase me in knowledge.* (20:114)

elation assigned to Jibril was the announcement to Maryam
(r.a.), the mother of Prophet Isa *(a.s.)*, of the impending birth of
her child. The archangel Mikail (Michael) *(a.s.)* is responsible for
the weather patterns created on earth. The archangel Azrail *(a.s.)*
takes the souls from their bodies at death and the archangel
Israfil *(a.s.)* is the blower of the trumpet on Judgment Day.

Archangels take their original form from the properties of
light characterized by the *alam-i-jabbarut*. The other classes of
angels derive theirs from the *alam-i-malakut*, the third created
realm. Because of the relative lack of density of light/matter in
these worlds, the bodies of angels have a fluid constitution. They
can therefore assume shapes appropriate for work in denser
worlds as well. That is why they sometimes appear on earth in
human form, which is a more comfortable and comprehensible
configuration to human perception.[2] Angels' forms change to fit
their function, as, for example, at the time of death, when a tun-
nel of light has been perceived by many who have returned to
describe this experience. It is said that the light-tunnel is the
form assumed by Archangel Azrail *(a.s.)* to take the soul back to
its Creator.

Allah created some angels to provide a light barrier between
Allah's Throne, or command post, and the lower worlds, while
others' sole function is to circle the Throne in an unceasing
litany of praise. Some angels are sent to earth in leagues to provide help on a large scale such as war; others are created as
guardians to individual human beings. There are angels who are
occupied only with recording the deeds of humans, others act as

---

[2] *And our messengers came to Ibrahim with good news. They said: Peace! He
answered: Peace! and delayed not to bring a roasted calf. And when he saw their
hands reached not to it, he mistrusted them and felt fearful of them. They said:
Fear not! Behold! we are sent to the folk of Lut.* (11:69, 70)

conduits for Allah's magnetism in facilitating consequences of His beneficence or wrath. Some angels act as witnesses during the prayers of the faithful. There are angels who assemble the masses at the Day of Judgment, while others are the keepers of the doors of paradise and hell.

One of the main tenets of Islam is belief in Allah's angels, with whom we share essential substance. *Alam-i-malakut,* the angels' abode, corresponds to the *seyrani ruh* in man, the soul which communicates between the material soul, or *jismani ruh,* and the souls which are closer to Allah's essence. This "moving soul" operates much like the angels who are moving in constant errands of aid or communication, dispatched by Allah to the material world of human beings.

Behold! We revealed it on the Night of Power. And what will convey to you what the Night of Power is! The Night of Power is better than a thousand months. The angels and the Spirit descend therein, by the permission of their Lord, on all errands. Peace until the rising of the dawn! (97)

One of the most blessed days for Sufis and all Muslims alike is the *Laylatul Qadr,* the Night of Power. It is customary for Sufi *tariqas* to hold *zikr* during this night towards the end of the holy month of *Ramadan,* because Allah sends His angels with extraordinary blessings, tidings of forgiveness, and revelatory messages. *Laylatul Qadr* is an opportunity for all believers to join with our angelic brethren in resounding the praises of the Creator, who opens up special lines of intercession through the angels on our behalf.

The Jinn

I created the jinn and humankind only that they might worship Me. (51:56)

Like the angels, jinn inhabit the *alam-i-malakut*. In terms of physical constitution the jinn are similar to angels, but their temperaments and habits are much closer to human beings. Like humans, jinn are endowed with free will and discrimination. Having the ability to make moral choices opens alternatives for jinn and humans to live righteously or not, an option unavailable to angels.

The bodies of human beings and jinn, as well as angels, each exist along a continuum of light/matter. The major difference between humans and jinn is their range of physical activity and perception based on their respective fields of vibration, which is determined by their physical habitat along the light/matter continuum. In other words, the light which shapes the human body is more "frozen" than the light of angels or jinn.[3] Whereas the human body is made of earth or clay, the jinn body is made of an electricity-like fire[4]. Because their self-awareness is not tempered by the quality of humility inherent in the earth, from which human beings are made, jinn have a tendency to haughtiness or pride. This attitude is furthered by their lightening-quick predisposition, a fiery nature which corresponds to the human being's *nafs*. Like humans, jinn were created with a *nafs* and also with the mental and spiritual apparatus suitable for understanding the complexities of Allah's being.

---

[3] For insight into recent scientific theories about the nature of light and matter, see Gough and Shacklett, "What Science Can and Can't Say About Spirits" (San Rafael, CA), 1999.

[4] *And the jinn did We create aforetime of essential fire.* (15:27)

*O company of jinn and men, if you have power to penetrate (all)
regions of the heavens and the earth, then penetrate (them)! You
will never penetrate them except with (Our) permission.* (55:33)

Jinn share with human beings the potential to achieve loving
intimacy with the Creator, who charged Prophet Muhammad
(a.s.) with bringing to them His message of truth. There are believing jinn and non-believers, Sufis and non-Sufis. Jinn, like humans,
were created to worship Allah, to strive for knowledge of His reality. Because Allah is just, jinn who wish to reach conscious union
with the Creator must, like humans, fight their *jihadu nafs*[5]. The
path of *tasawwuf* which Allah bequeathed to Muhammad is open
to willing jinn. Certain Sufi *shaykhs* have orders to represent the
Prophet in *tariqa* specifically for jinn *murids*.

Jinn have families, live in tribes and have leaders, much like
humanity. They are beset by the same concerns as man, namely, to
live life fully and well. Because they operate at a much higher level
of vibrational frequency than human beings, jinn have the ability
to invade the more solid matter of earthly objects and beings,
including animals and humans. Their natural curiosity and play-
fulness tempts some of the less enlightened among the jinn to
abuse this invasive ability. They derive a kind of vicarious enjoy-
ment by prompting verbal remarks or behavior in human beings,
because they do not have the characteristics of a solid constitution
which would allow them to do so naturally. An analogous situation in human society is a person who steals a race car and drives
it very fast, regardless of the danger to himself, the car, or others
on the road. If he could personally move as fast as that race car, the

---

[5] *Jihadu nafs*: holy war against selfish desires, which the Prophet *(a.s.)* called,
"the big *jihad*."

incentive for him to steal one would diminish considerably.

Among preferred targets of opportunistic jinn are mentally unstable people and those with a perverted spirituality or moral deficit. Human beings have a natural magnetic energy shield surrounding their body which acts as a protective barrier against negative vibrational intrusion. People suffering from mental or moral imbalance undergo a weakening of this shield, or aura, which produces gaps in the protective energy. Mischievous jinn see this as an opportunity to enter the human's body and amuse themselves by performing ridiculous antics or uttering offensive or nonsensical statements through their host. Many people misinterpret this type of jinn invasion as Satanic possession.

Some people commune with spirits for information from the "other side." Unfortunately, in many cases these people may be unknowing conduits for jinn, who may provide inaccurate information or even deliberate misinformation. The fact that jinn are able to manipulate themselves around a variety of dimensional levels does not mean that they are omniscient or omnipotent beings. Without having a good reason and specific permission to attempt to communicate with jinn, it is advisable to avoid contact with them for at least two reasons: one, jinn energy and human energy are not very compatible and humans are likely to be harmed by much interaction, and two, the unruly beings among them can be formidable and unscrupulous opponents for the spiritually unprotected.

Shaytan

And (remember) when We said to the angels: Fall prostrate before Adam, and they fell prostrate, all except Iblis. He was of the jinn, so he rebelled against his Lord's command. Will you choose him

and his progeny for your protecting friends instead of Me, when
they are your enemy? Disastrous is the exchange for evil-doers.
(18:50)

There is a jinn named Shaytan (Satan), who was once close
to Allah, having beheld many of the secrets of creation. He was
present when Allah created the human being, and therefore pre-
ceded him in knowledge. Shaytan's arrogance, however, was his
downfall in that it prevented him from obeying the Creator
when he was told to bow down before Adam. His argument was
that Adam was made of lowly clay, while he was made of much
superior fire. His attitude was gravely offensive to Allah, who
only asked the angels and Shaytan to prostrate after He had
blown His spirit into Adam's body. In refusing to bow to Adam,
Shaytan was refusing to bow to Allah. Such an overt rebellion
against the Creator was tantamount to setting himself up as
equal to Allah, an unpardonable offense.

He said: My Lord! Because You have sent me astray, I verily
shall adorn the path of error for them in the earth, and shall
mislead them every one, except those who are Your perfectly
devoted slaves. He said: This is a straight way to Me! For over
any of My slaves you have no power except those who choose to
follow you. (15:39-42)

This conversation between Allah and Shaytan highlights the
character of this rebellious jinn. His intention is to mislead
Allah's creatures, but Allah gives him permission to mislead only
those who have chosen to follow him. Thus the person who
chooses the route of disobedience to Allah is held responsible for
his actions, for Shaytan was never given authority to force any-

one into disbelief. Further, Allah restricts Shaytan's role by denying him power over any of His believing servants.

A true understanding of the role assumed by Shaytan at the beginning of the creation of man should bolster the resolve of a believer who wishes to become closer to Allah. Sufis take literally the statement, "*La hawla wa la quwwata ila billahi ul Ali ul Azim*"—"There is no power or strength except Allah's, the High, the Mighty." Shaytan is not the Prince of Darkness, Ruler of Evil. Allah's dominion is all-inclusive, and therefore not a thing can occur without His knowledge and permission. Out of His *Jalal* side, He created the potential for evil, the opposite of Himself, when He allowed His creatures the power of choice. Should their choices be based on the faulty notion that they are not beholden to their Creator, Allah allows Shaytan to help them along the way to perdition. Always, however, it is Allah's power of guidance at work.

The crucial point here is that the onus falls on us to choose the path pleasing to Allah, and to forego the path which, although created by Allah, brings Allah's wrath[6]. When we do err, Allah in His attribute of *Al-Ghaffar*, The Forgiving, is ever at the ready to overlook our mistakes when we commit a wrong in ignorance, or if we humble ourselves in sincere repentance for acknowledged wrongdoing. Shaytan made no such effort to correct himself and remained unabashed, whereas Adam admitted his intransigence in the garden of Eden and was consequently given his entire lifetime to make amends.

---

[6] Allah teaches us how to ask for His help to choose correctly in the first *Sura* of Quran, *Al Fatiha*: *Show us the straight path, the path of those whom You have favored; Not the path of those who earn Your wrath nor of those who go astray.* (1:5-7)

And call not on any other god besides Allah. There is no god but He.
Everything will perish except His countenance. His is the command,
and to Him you will be brought back. (28:88)

The human being is perched at the fulcrum of *Al-Adl*, the
Creator's name The Just One, as the activator of Allah's attributes
of mercy and wrath. The well-balanced representation of these
divine traits, based on humble submission to the Owner of all, is
what distinguishes the wise from the spiritually unconscious.
The *insan-i-kamil* understands his divine purpose and has come
full circle in his journey from the essence of Allah back to his origin. He made his debut on earth as an infant knowing nothing,
experienced the folly of incomplete knowledge in his *nafs*-driven
self, and has finally learned the truth in his state of complete surrender to Allah. Like an infant, he knows not a thing, but has
been made privy to the secret that all knowledge is with Allah,
that all existence is Allah. With a deep understanding of the affirmation of faith, *"La ilaha illa 'llah,"* the consummate Sufi lives
in a universe held together by the pure love of Allah, and is
amazed at the spectacle.

Glossary of Terms

Abdal: Plural of **badal**.

Adab: Good manners; courteous behavior; the way to act.

Ahlak: Personal character or temperament.

Alam-i-jabbarut: The world, or realm, of the **archangels**.

Alam-i-lahut: The world, or realm, of the essence of Allah.

Alam-i-malakut: The world, or realm, of the **angels**.

Alam-i-mulk: The world, or realm, of creation.

Aleyhi salam: "Peace be upon him"; an honorific phrase traditionally uttered after mentioning the name of a **prophet** or **archangel**; abbr. a.s.

Alim: Knower, in a scholarly sense.

Amri maruf: The encouragement of good deeds.

Anbiya Al Mursalin: Prophet-Messengers.

Angel: A being created for the express purpose of carrying out Allah's commands.

Aql: The rational mind.

Archangel: An **angel** with superior powers and responsibility.

Arif: Knower, according to deep spiritual states; gnostic.

Azrael: The **archangel** who takes the souls from their bodies at death.

Ayn-al-Yaqin: Lit., the eye of undeniably sure knowledge; apprehension of sure knowledge by way of personal experience and observation.

Badal: Substitute; a **wali** who is in such a state of surrender to Allah that he performs divine duties spontaneously; a minister to the **qutb**.

Bakabillah: Lit., being constant in Allah.

Beautiful Names: See **Most Beautiful Names**.

Bektashi: Name of a widely known Sufi **tariqa** founded by Haji Bektash Wali (1281-1338 C.E.); a Sufi who belongs to the Bektashi Tariqa.

Beloved: An appellation of Allah particularly meaningful to Sufis.

Biat: Pledge of allegiance; solemn vow taken between a Sufi initiate and his **shaykh**.

Bismillah er Rahman er Rahim: Lit., "In the name of God, the Most Merciful, the Most Compassionate", known as the Basmallah.

Confession of Unity: "La ilaha illa 'llah." ("There is no god but God").

Dajjal: the evil misleader; the Antichrist.

Dedeghan: Elders or senior members of a Sufi **tariqa**.

Dergah: Gathering place; place where **zikr** and **sohbet** are held.

Dervish: A student of Sufism; a degree of advancement in a Sufi student.

Ehli samawat: People of the heavens.

Fana: Dissolving; merging; ending.

Fanaful Pir: Dissolving in the **Pir**.

Fanaful Rasul: Dissolving in the Messenger *(a.s.)*.

Fanaful Shaykh: Dissolving in the **Shaykh**.

Fanafullah: Dissolving in Allah.

Gaffar: Able to forgive.

Gawsul Azam: The Greatest Helper; an honorific title referring to the Sufi saint and founder of the Qadiri **Tariqa** Hazreti Abdul Qadir Geylani *(r.a.)* which describes his power of intercession on behalf of the believer.

Gospel: The scripture sent to Prophet Isa *(a.s.)*.

Habibullah: The lover of Allah; Allah's beloved.

Hadith: Lit., tradition; well-known anecdote concerning the actions and sayings of Prophet Muhammad *(a.s.)* as based on eyewitness accounts; also known as **Qudsi-Hadith**; *hadiths* is a compilation of such anecdotes.

Hadrat: See **Hazreti**.

Hal: A temporary spiritual state, as opposed to **maqam**, which is a permanent spiritual station.

Halal: Permissible, according to sacred law, or **sharia**.

Halvet: Spiritual retreat.

Haqiqa: The state of knowing absolute truth.

Haqq-al-Yaqin: Lit., the truth of undeniably sure knowledge; apprehension of sure knowledge directly from Allah within the heart.

Haram: Forbidden, according to sacred law, or **sharia**.

Hazreti: The Great; an honorific title (abbr. Hz.).

Ijaza: The license to teach Sufism.

Ilm-al-Yaqin: Lit., the knowledge of undeniably sure knowledge; apprehension of sure knowledge by way of written or verbal communication.

Insan-i-Kamil: The perfected human being.

Irfan: Gnosis; inner knowing.

Irshad: Teaching the way to enlightenment.

Ishq: Ardent love.

Ismi Jalal: Lit., the Name of Might, i.e., "Allah."

Israfil: the **archangel** who will "blow the trumpet" on Judgment Day.

Jahri zikr: Ceremonial remembrance of Allah executed in such a way as to be audible to others.

Jalal: Lit., Might; Allah's attributes of power or wrath.

Jamal: Lit., Beauty; Allah's attributes of mercy.

Jibril: The **archangel** whose responsibilities include conveying messages and scriptures from Allah to His prophets and other saintly people; known also as Gabriel.

Jihad: Holy war.

Jihadu nafs: The holy war against one's ego or self.

Jinn: Non-human being who is comprised of an electricity-like form of energy and is not visible to the ordinary human eye.

Jismani Ruh: Lit., corporeal soul; one of the composite of four human souls; the soul whose substance issues forth from the life-force of Allah.

Kaaba: The house of Allah in Mecca, originally built by Adam *(a.s.)*, rebuilt by Ibrahim *(a.s.)*, and rededicated by Muhammad *(a.s.)*; the sacred destination of Muslim pilgrims.

Kabbala: Judaic mysticism.

Khafi zikr: Ceremonial remembrance of Allah executed in such a way as to be audible only to oneself.

La hawla wa la quwwata ila billahi ul Ali ul Azim: "There is no power or strength except in Allah, the High, the Mighty."

La ilaha illa 'llah: "There is no god but God"; the Muslim declaration of faith; the affirmation of the oneness of Allah.

Laylatul Qadr: Night of Power, observed annually on one of the last ten days of the Muslim month of Ramadan, during which Allah sends **angels** with special blessings to mankind.

Malak: Lit., having the power and ability to do deeds; **Angel**.

Maqam: Station; spiritual level.

Marifa: State of knowing; state of Muhammad's *(a.s.)* understanding.

Messenger: An envoy, who also may be a prophet or an **angel**, sent by Allah to convey a message to humanity and/or jinn.

Mevlevi: Name of a widely known Sufi **tariqa** founded by followers of Mevlana Jalaluddin Rumi (1207-1273 C.E.); a Sufi who belongs to the Mevlevi Tariqa.

Mikhail: The **archangel** whose responsibilities and powers include managing weather patterns on earth; also known as Michael.

Miraj: See entry below.

Miraj-i-manawi: Prophet Muhammad's *(a.s.)* famed spiritual Night Journey in which he visited sacred sites on earth and traversed the heavens; spiritual journey taken by Sufis after completion of the process of **tasawwuf**.

Most Beautiful Names: The attributes by which Allah describes Himself.

Murid: Sufi student; the one who surrenders his will and power to Allah.

Murshid: Lit., one who enlightens; teacher; Sufi master.

Mutasadduq: The charitable one.

Nafs: Lit., breath; egoistic nature; man's animal nature; the whole man as an individual being.

Nahy-i-munkar: The discouraging of ill deeds.

Naqshbandi: Name of a widely known Sufi **tariqa** founded by Bahauddin Naqshbandi (1318-1389 C.E.); a Sufi who belongs to the Naqshbandi Tariqa.

Ninety-Nine Names: See Most Beautiful Names.

Nur-i-Muhammad: the Light of Muhammad; the first created entity.

Pir: Spiritual ancestor; founder of a Sufi **tariqa**; living principal of a Sufi **tariqa**.

Prophet: A designated representative of Allah, whose mission on earth was to enlighten mankind as to spiritual truth, dispense Allah's power as needed, and warn mankind of imminent consequences for their wrongdoing; one of the keepers of the covenant between mankind and Allah; *The* Prophet refers to Muhammad of Arabia *(a.s.)*.

Psalms: A scripture revealed to Prophet David *(a.s.)* in the form of a compilation of devotional lyric verses.

Qadiri: Name of a widely known Sufi **tariqa** founded by Abdul Qadir Geylani (1078-1166 C.E.); a Sufi who belongs to the Qadiri Tariqa.

Qudsi-Hadith: Lit., Holy Tradition; a documented eyewitness account of a saying or action of Prophet Muhammad *(a.s.)*; also known as Hadiths-i-Qudsi or **hadith**.

Quran: Lit., recitation or lecture; the holy scripture revealed to Prophet Muhammad *(a.s.)* over the course of twenty-three years; the last scripture revealed to mankind.

Qutb: Lit., pole; a person of extremely high spiritual level who acts as administrator in the spiritual hierarchy of the world; a conduit of spiritual power from Allah, through whom it is distributed in the world.

Qutb al Zaman: The Supreme Qutb; the living head of the spiritual administration.

Rabita: Spiritual connection between a person and Allah, or between two people; a Sufi practice of purposeful spiritual connection between a **shaykh** and his student.

Radiyallahu anh: "May Allah be pleased with him"; an honorific phrase traditionally uttered after mentioning the name of one of the Prophet's *(a.s.)* **Khalifas** or a great saint; abbr. r.a.

Rafiq: Extreme softness of character.

Rifai: Name of a widely known Sufi **tariqa** founded by Ahmed er Rifai (1120-1183 C.E.); a Sufi who belongs to the Rifai Tariqa.

Ruh: Spirit; soul.

Ruhani Ruh: Lit., the holy spirit; one of the composite of four human souls; the soul whose substance issues forth from the essence of Allah.

Sadiq: One who is loyal.

Safa: A state of spiritual tranquility.

Safabillah: Lit., being eternally happy with Allah.

Sahabe: Lit., companions; Prophet Muhammad's early followers, who accompanied him in his daily life for spiritual enrichment and to be at his disposal to provide any needed service.

Sajjada: Prayer rug; a small rug on which Muslims traditionally offer ritual prayer five times daily.

Salik: A spiritual seeker.

Sattar: Covering another's shame; hiding others' faults from themselves and the public; concealing another's shortcomings.

Sayrifullah: Lit., journeying in Allah.

Sayrima'Allah: Lit., journeying with Allah.

Sefiroth: Divine attributes which emanate from the unified Being of God throughout the universe, according to the **Kabbala**, a body of Jewish mystical doctrine; spiritual perception points in the human body which correspond to divine attributes in the universe, e.g., mercy and judgment.

Seyrani Ruh: Lit., moving soul; one of the composite of four human souls; the soul whose substance issues from the realm of **angels**, dreams, and **jinn**.

Seyyid: A descendent of Prophet Muhammad *(a.s.)*.

Shafiq: Extreme kindness.

Sharia: The body of Islamic religious canons.

Shaykh: Commonly used in the Middle East as an honorific title, to signify elder, teacher, tribal leader; authorized teacher of **tasawwuf**.

Siddiq: One who is truthful; an honorific title usually reserved for Abu Bakr *(r.a.)*, the Prophet Muhammad's *(a.s.)* friend and **Khalifa**.

Silsila: The chain of spiritual lineage.

Sohbet: A divinely inspired talk given by a **shaykh** among his students.

Sufism: Modern Western term for **tasawwuf**, the system of spiritual cleansing practiced by Sufis.

Sultani Ruh: Lit., divine soul; one of the composite of four human souls; the soul whose substance issues from the spiritual realm of the **archangels**.

Suluk: The path of a seeker; the particular life's course or path of each student of Sufism; the sum of experiences, both spiritual and mundane, in the life of a student of Sufism.

Sunna: Observed behavior of the Prophet *(a.s.)*.

Sura: One of the one-hundred fourteen sections of Quran, roughly translated as "chapter."

Tafakkur: Meditative contemplation.

Tajallay-i-sirr: The spiritual state of knowing the secret of creation.

Tajallay-i-sirrul sirr: The spiritual state of knowing the secret of the secret of creation.

Talqin: Inculcation; the practice of deliberate mental self-conditioning.

Taqwa: Avoiding sins; fearing Allah.

Tariqa: Lit., path; the Sufi path, or school of spiritual study; the path to Allah as exemplified in the behavior of Prophet Muhammad *(a.s.)*; a particular Sufi school, or order.

Tasarruf: Executive spiritual power; a **shaykh**'s authority to exercise spiritual power at his discretion.

Tasawwuf: The system of spiritual cleansing known in the West as Sufism.

Tawba: Repentance.

Torah: The first five Books of the Old Testament, also known as the Pentateuch.

Vicegerent: A representative appointed by a sovereign ruler to exercise executive power in his name; viceregent.

Wali: Lit., Protecting Friend, one of **Allah's Beautiful Names** or attributes; a Sufi who has attained a high spiritual level, on which Allah has bestowed this attribute.

Waliullah: Lit., Friend of Allah; an honorific title usually reserved for Ali ibn Abi Talib *(r.a.)*, Prophet Muhammad's *(a.s.)* cousin and designated representative.

Wazifa: Personal practice whereby a student of Sufism repeatedly invokes the attributes of Allah according to a formula prescribed by his teacher; individual **zikr**.

Wilayat: The state of protective friendship, a spiritual level attained by a Sufi on whom Allah has bestowed His attribute *Al-Wali*, the Protecting Friend.

Yaqin: Undeniably sure knowledge.

Zat: Essence or person of a being.

Zikr: Remembrance; traditional Sufi liturgy, exercised both congregationally and individually.

Suggested Reading and References

Scriptures and Hadiths:

The Holy Qur-'aan. Transliteration in Roman Script (With Original Arabic Text) by Mohammad Abdul Haleem Eliasii, English translation by Mohammed Marmaduke Pickthall. Charminar Hyderabad-India: Eliasii Family Book Service, 1996.

The Holy Qur-an. Text, Translation and Commentary by Abdullah Yusuf Ali. Lahore, 1934. Reprint, N.P.: The Muslim Students' Association of the United States and Canada, 1975.

The Five Books of Moses. A New Translation with Introductions, Commentary, and Notes by Everett Fox. New York: Shocken Books Inc., distributed by Pantheon Books, a division of Random House, Inc., New York, 1995.

The Other Bible. Ancient Alternative Scriptures, Edited with Introductions by Willis Barnstone. New York: Harper Collins, HarperSanFrancisco, 1984.

Sahih Al-Boukhari. the Traditions of Sayings and Doings of the Prophet Muhammad …, by Imam Al-Boukhari, English trans. from original Arabic by Dr. Mahmoud Matraji, collected and revised by F. Amira Zrein Matraji. Beirut: Dar El Fiker, 1993.

The Beauty of the Righteous and Ranks of the Elite: A Collection of … Accounts Based on … Hilyat-ul Awliya Wa Tabaqat al-Asfiya. Trans. From the Original Arabic and Edited by Shaykh Muhammad Al-Akili. Philadelphia: Pearl Publishing House, 1995.

Sufi Teachings by Hz. Abdul Qadir Geylani:

Al-Jilani, Shaikh 'Abd Al-Qadir, The Sublime Revelation (Al-Fath ar-Rabbani): A Collection of Sixty-Two Discourses, translated from the Arabic by Muhtar Holland. Houston: Al-Baz Publishing, Inc., 1992.
—**Revelations of the Unseen (Futuh al-Ghaib):** A Collection of Seventy-Eight Discourses, trans. from the Ar. by Muhtar Holland. Houston: Al-Baz Publishing, Inc., 1992.
—**Utterances (Malfuzat).** Trans. from the Ar. by Muhtar Holland. Houston: Al-Baz Publishing, Inc., 1992.

General Spiritual Topics and Biographies:

'Ata ur-Rahim, Muhammad, Jesus, Prophet of Islam. Elmhurst, NY: Tahrike Tarsile Qur'an, Inc., 1991.
Lings, Martin, Muhammad. New York: Inner Traditions International, Ltd., 1983.
Poncé, Charles, Kabbalah: An Introduction and Illumination for the World Today. Wheaton, IL: The Theosophical Publishing House, Quest Books, 1973.
Raza, M. Shamim, Introducing the Prophets. Lahore: Sh. Muhammad Ashraf, 1973.

Articles on general Sufi topics can be found in **Call of the Divine**, the journal/newsletter of the Qadiri Rifai Tariqa. Napa, CA: Ansari Publications, 1993-2000.

Science/Spirituality:

Hawking, Stephen, A Brief History of Time: From the Big Bang to Black Holes, introduction by Carl Sagan. New York: Bantam Books, 1988.

The following is a brief listing of references and related articles prepared under the auspices of the Foundation for Mind-Being Research, President William C. Gough. For further information they may be contacted at PO Box 449, Los Altos, CA 94023-0449, (650) 941-7462, http://fmbr.org

Gough, William C., "Developing a Bridge Between Science and Sufism," Sufism: An Inquiry, Journal of the International Association of Sufism, Vol. 6: 4, 1997, pp.26-37; also published in the Proceedings of the Fourth Annual Sufism Symposium, held in Newark/Fremont, CA, March 7-9, 1997. An expanded version entitled, "Science and Sufism" was published in the Fourteenth International Conference on the Study of Shamanism and Alternate Modes of Healing, Santa Sabina Center, San Rafael, CA, Aug. 30-Sept.1, 1997, pp.13-21.

—**"The Cellular Communication Process and Alternative Modes of Healing**," Subtle Energies and Energy Medicine, Vol. 8: 2, 1997, pp.67-101; also published in the Proceedings of the Fifteenth International conference on the Study of Shamanism and Alternate Modes of Healing, San Rafael, CA, Sept. 5-7, 1998.

Gough, William C. and Robert L. Shacklett, "The Science of Connectiveness: Part I, Modeling a Greater Unity; Part II, Mapping Beyond Space-Time, and Part III, The Human Experience," Subtle Energies and Energy Medicine, Journal of the International Society for the Study of Subtle Energies and Energy Medicine, Vol. 4: 1,2,3, 1993, pp. 57-76, 99-123, 187-214.

—**"Outer and Inner Light**," Proceedings of the Twelfth International Conference on the Study of Shamanism and Alternate Modes of Healing, San Rafael, CA, Sept. 2-4, 1995; also published in the Journal of Religion and Psychical Research, Vol. 20:2, April, 1997, pp.64-83.

—**"Keys to an Expanded Scientific Paradigm**," Proceedings of the Thirteenth International Conference on the Study of Shamanism and Alternate Modes of Healing, San Rafael, CA, Aug. 31-Sept. 2, 1996, pp.32-48.

—**"What Science Can and Can't Say About Spirits**," Proceedings of the Sixteenth International Conference on Shamanism and Alternate Modes of Healing, San Rafael, CA, Sept. 4 - 6,1999. (To be published as a three-part series in The Journal of Religion and Psychical Research, in the July, 2000, Oct., 2000, and Jan., 2001 issues.)

Acknowledgments

We are grateful for those who have contributed in the publishing of this book in memory of a deceased loved one.

In memory of:
Bill and Betty Brown
Reverend Benjamin T. Clark
Rashid Mustafa Salim
Beatrice D. F. Stromwasser
Mildred Stromwasser
Kamilunnisa Fatima Muhsina Tobis

Other contributors:
Nusrat and Abdul Hai Rajput

OR

Ete kemiğe büründüm
Yunus diye göründüm

I wrapped myself in bone and flesh

and appeared as "Yunus."

—Yunus Emre
(c. 1240-1320 C.E.)

In Turkey, during the thirteenth century, two great Sufi poets lived and worked. Mevlana Jelaluddin Rumi was the more prolific of the two, well known for his volumes of inspired masterpieces. Yunus Emre wrote simpler lyric pieces which were often set to music. One day the two met, and Mevlana showed his colleague his latest work. At length, after Yunus had studied the copious volume, Mevlana asked him,

"Well, what do you think?"

Yunus thought for a moment and declared, "You said too much."

"What should I have said?" asked Mevlana.

Yunus replied, "If I were you, I would have put it like this, I wrapped myself in bone and flesh and appeared as 'Yunus.'"

Es-Seyyid Es-Shaykh Taner Mustafa Ansari Tarsusi er Rifai el Qadiri

About the Author

Es-Seyyid Es-Shaykh Taner Mustafa Ansari Tarsusi er Rifai el Qadiri was born in Tarsus, Turkey, to a devout Muslim family of Seyyids, descendants of Prophet Muhammad. He completed his university studies in Michigan, where he helped found the Muslim Students Association of the United States and Canada. He was initiated into the Qadiri Rifai Tariqa in Istanbul under Shaykh Muhyiddin Ansari, from whom he received his license to teach Sufism; his spiritual lineage also includes the Naqshbandi, Mevlevi, and Bektashi orders. Shaykh Taner accepted leadership of the Qadiri Rifai Tariqa of the Americas after the passing of Shaykh Muhyiddin's successor, Shaykh Nuruddin Ozal. He teaches Sufism throughout the United States and abroad. Shaykh Taner regularly publishes articles on spiritual topics, and is currently working on his third book on Sufism. He resides in California, where he teaches privately and holds regular lectures and zikr, the congregational Sufi service.

About the Editor

Elizabeth Muzeyyen Brown has been a student of Shaykh Taner Ansari since 1993, and has collaborated with the Shaykh as editor of his articles on Sufism for several years. Ms. Brown holds a Bachelor of Music degree from Temple University in Philadelphia, and has pursued postgraduate instrumental studies in Cuba and Turkey. She is currently working with Shaykh Taner on a book of Sufi stories.

What About My Wood?
101 True Sufi Stories

As told by
Es-Seyyid Es-Shaykh
Taner Ansari Tarsusi er Rifai el Qadiri

Coming January 2001

Rain

A Sufi was traveling and came upon a village, which had been experiencing a drought. When the people of the village saw this bearded man approaching, they recognized him as a religious person. Feeling that the traveler must have a very close relationship with Allah, the villagers gathered around him, asking him to pray for rain.

The Sufi wanted to help them and replied, "Very well, then. Please bring me a bucket of water."

When the water was brought to him, he took his coat off and soaked it thoroughly. He then laid it out on a large rock and found a spot nearby to sit down to wait for his coat to dry.

The villagers watched this Sufi with amazement. They could not believe that he was wasting their precious drinking water this way. However, they said nothing to their visitor, and sat down with him, as they had nothing better to do.

After a time, it looked as if the coat might be dry, so the Sufi got up to check it. Just then, it began to rain very hard. The Sufi sighed and picked up his drenched coat.

As he started to walk away, the villagers stopped him and asked, "What happened? We didn't see you praying. All you did was wash your coat."

The Sufi replied, "Allah and I are not getting along very well these days. I figured that if I wished for something, Allah would do the opposite. So I got a wet coat. You got your rain."

Traveling with Your Shaykh

One day Ali Baba's shaykh remarked to him, "Bursa is nice these days."

Ali Baba understood his shaykh to mean that he should go to Bursa, knowing the subtle way that Sufis communicate. Ali Baba, in a state of surrender to his shaykh, decided to travel to Bursa, but he didn't have a car, or a horse, or even a donkey, and Bursa was 600 miles away! So he did what he could and surrendered the rest to Allah.

He rolled a bed, went to the train station and waited.

He thought, "I did my job. I'm here. This is all that I can do." (In fact, his bed roll only caused him problems on his journey because he had to carry it everywhere even though he did not even once use it.)

After he had been waiting at the station for some time, Ali Baba saw smoke coming from a train, which was about ten kilometers away.

At that moment a stranger approached him and asked, "Did you buy a ticket?"

Ali Baba answered, "No. I do not have any money to buy a ticket."

The man bought him a ticket and sent him on his way to Bursa.

When Ali Baba returned, his shaykh asked him, "Ali Baba did you go to Bursa and come back?"

Ali Baba replied, "Yes, my Shaykh, you took me there and you brought me back."

The Idiot Dervish

There was once a shaykh who had many dervishes. This shaykh treated his dervishes very well. Although they had to work hard to serve their shaykh, they were happy to do so. Their shaykh fed and clothed them, took them on trips and showed them all manner of Allah's wonders. He even let them sleep in his house.

But there was one idiot dervish to whom the shaykh seemed not to pay much attention. Although the shaykh fed this dervish, the bread was always a little stale. And the clothes that he wore were always hand-me-downs. He often had to sleep out on the porch in the rain, for lack of space inside the shaykh's house. When the shaykh and his dervishes went on trips, this poor dervish stayed home. Sometimes he cried from loneliness.

Passersby would tease this idiot dervish, calling him a fool for putting up with such rough treatment. They laughed at him and said that his shaykh did not love him; how could he love him when he treated him this way?

The dervish simply protested, saying that his shaykh truly loved him the most. He left them with these words, "There is no bread, there are no clothes, there is no rain. There is only my shaykh."

Between the Loved and the Beloved
Poems & Sayings

Es-Seyyid, Es-Shaykh
Taner Ansari Tarsusi er Rifai el Qadiri

Revised and Expanded Edition
Coming January 2001

Wheat and Sufi

ne grain of wheat and one Sufi.
Grain is planted in the Earth.
So is Sufi.
Grain sprouts out from earth.
So does Sufi.
Grain is reaped.
So is Sufi.
Grain goes to the mill.
So does Sufi.
Grain is stepped on, crushed, ground.
So is Sufi.
Grain goes to the baker.
So does Sufi.
Grain, flour, dough, so is Sufi.
Then comes the oven.
Grain is baked, cooked.
So is Sufi.
Grain becomes bread, well respected,
Cooked for nourishing.
So is Sufi.
Grain becomes a man who joins the man.
So does Sufi.

Boxing Match

I thought hitting the other guy is winning the match. I learned that winning the match is how much hitting I can take before the other guy gives up.

Death is losing your identity.

Dying before you die is losing your identity in this body.

Being reborn is attaining Allah's identity.

Only with Allah's identity you live forever.